Jean,

Good luck with the
assignment.

Kindy regards

Robert Walls

EU
Structural Funds
and Other
Public Sector
Investments

EU
Structural Funds and Other Public Sector Investments

A Guide to Evaluation Methods

Alan W. Gray

Gill & Macmillan

Gill & Macmillan Ltd
Goldenbridge
Dublin 8

with associated companies throughout the world

© Alan W. Gray 1995

0 7171 2242 5

Index compiled by Helen Litton
Designed by Typeform Repro Ltd, Dublin
Printed in Ireland by ColourBooks Ltd, Dublin

A catalogue record is available for this book from the British Library.

1   3   5   4   2

For Albert and Sadie

CONTENTS

LIST OF EXAMPLES

LIST OF CHARTS

PREFACE

Arising from the Single European Act there will be a dramatic increase in European structural and cohesion fund expenditures. The structural funds have been reorganised and expanded. Much of the funds are administered within agreed Community Support Frameworks. In the second round (1994–99) the size of these funds will amount to 149.8 billion ECU in 1994 prices. In addition, the new Cohesion Fund will involve the spending of 16 billion ECU. The funds will be concentrated in the least prosperous regions of the European Union countries, the main beneficiaries being Spain, Portugal, Greece, Italy, and Ireland, though all member-states will receive some benefit.

A key issue of relevance to the European Commission and to all the member-states is how effective the use of these expenditures will be. This is relevant both to the more prosperous countries, where taxpayers are ultimately funding these expenditures, and to the poorer regions, where the funds may represent the last opportunity to improve their economic performance significantly. Much of the funds are likely to be allocated to investment projects, and the key issue will be the economic return on these investments.

A practical problem facing the EU countries and their advisers is how to evaluate proposed investment expenditures. The same issues arise in relation to other public sector investments that are funded by national taxpayers. This task is made more difficult by the fact that not only are there no consistent methods of appraisal for public sector investments between member-states but even within individual countries, different approaches and different assumptions are used in the evaluation of proposed investments.

Inappropriate and inconsistent methods for evaluating investment decisions on the use of structural and cohesion fund expenditures open up the real possibility that investments will be made where the returns will be negative or lower than alternative possibilities. The same applies to other exchequer-funded investment decisions. Such an outcome would damage the prospects for economic growth in Europe and would have a negative impact on individual living standards and employment opportunities.

This book attempts to make a contribution to the difficult objective of maximising the economic return on European structural fund investments and other public sector investments by providing a practical guide to the methods of investment appraisal. The issues dealt with are also relevant to decisions concerning private sector investment proposals that are being considered for assistance through EU structural funds or other public sector subsidies. This book represents an introduction to all the main issues involved in the evaluation of EU or other public sector expenditures. It also provides a practical guide to many of the operational tasks involved in undertaking such evaluations. The detailed bibliography will direct readers to other references that would assist in the task of considering how to carry out specific evaluations. A general policy-oriented reader who wishes to obtain an overview of the techniques and the pitfalls and basic steps involved may wish to skip chapters 3–5 and concentrate on chapters 1–2 and 6–8.

A number of examples are used in the text. These examples are not presented to indicate the findings on the areas covered but rather to highlight practical methodological issues.

ACKNOWLEDGMENTS

I would like to acknowledge the invaluable advice on practical aspects of the appraisal of public sector projects and programmes provided over a number of years by policy-makers and economists in EU member-states and in the European Commission, as well as policy-makers in Canada and in the United States. Valuable insights on investment appraisal of capital projects were also provided by a number of major commercial companies and financial institutions.

I would also like to acknowledge the advice given by Professor Patrick Honohan of the Economic and Social Research Institute in Dublin, who made suggestions on a previous draft, and my colleagues in Indecon. The usual disclaimer applies.

1

ISSUES AND APPROACHES TO EVALUATION

1.1 KEY ISSUES

The key issue facing policy-makers in the evaluation of public sector investment or expenditure programmes, whether funded by the European Union or by the national exchequer, is how to ensure that the best use will be made of the resources available.

This in turn require.

- that appropriate and consistent methods of appraisal are designed and implemented

- ensuring that individual projects are likely to make a net economic return

- that more attractive alternatives are not overlooked

- that the wider impact of investment decisions on the returns from other projects is also evaluated.

As the size of investments funded by EU structural funds expands, it is essential that effective methods of economic evaluation and planning are correctly applied. This necessity has been increasingly recognised following the negative returns evident in some investments in the past and as the economic impact of investments is more fully understood.

It is important that progress is made in applying methods of appraisal to proposed public sector investment decisions in EU countries and also that increased attention is paid to the evaluation of the results of previous investments and policy interventions. Feedback from the evaluation of the performance of previous projects can be very effective in improving decision-making and in refining the methods and techniques of evaluation.

1

It is also essential that analysts undertaking evaluations work closely with the decision-makers to ensure that there is 'ownership' of the findings so that there can be a real improvement in the returns from expenditure or investment programmes. Too often reports lie on the shelf rather than result in changes in the allocation of resources. This is as often due to the failure of the analyst to produce convincing and clearly understandable conclusions as it is to other causes.

Role of Different Levels of Authorities

A number of different types of authorities and organisations are likely to be involved in carrying out appraisals of public sector investments or expenditure programmes, including those financed by EU structural funds. These include the European Commission, national governments, regional and local authorities, state agencies, and organisations and enterprises wishing to secure EU funds for projects in the commercial sector. Governments and EU institutions have a central role in deciding where EU and other public expenditure funds should go.

There is an increasing focus on the role of sub-regional and community involvement in the allocation of structural funds. It is the author's view, however, that in general, evaluations of projects should be undertaken from a national or EU perspective and that the same techniques and types of analysis should be undertaken by all the different types of authorities and organisations involved. In many cases the impact of proposals on sub-regional or local communities should also be assessed, but this should represent additional information rather than an alternative to considering the national implications.

It is also important that where feasible, governments should establish price and other incentive signals to ensure that regional or local agencies and the commercial sector make the right investment decisions. For example, if prices were inappropriate because of distortions in the economy, the introduction of a government tax might mean that other agencies would not have to undertake a full economic appraisal of investment decisions, as a commercial or financial appraisal would be sufficient. Where this is not possible there should be national guidelines on the key macro-assumptions that should be used in specific evaluations. This issue is discussed in more detail in chapter 4.

As a result of the contribution of welfare economics there is growing acceptance of the importance of applying economic efficiency criteria to public sector investments and other elements of public expenditure. There has also been substantial progress in the development of a range of approaches to the evaluation of individual investment decisions as well as investment programmes. These are discussed below.

1.2 MAIN APPROACHES

The task of evaluating EU structural funds requires the same approach as in evaluating other public sector investments. This is a complex task where judgment cannot be replaced by the simplistic application of techniques; there are, however, a number of approaches that can be usefully applied in attempting to ensure that investment funds achieve the maximum possible economic return and contribute to sustainable economic development in EU countries.

There are four main types of analysis that can be carried out; each situation involving the evaluation of public expenditure programmes requires one or more of these approaches. The main approaches are:

- Strategic reviews
- Cost-effectiveness studies
- Financial appraisals
- Cost-benefit analysis

Applicability of Different Approaches

The merits of each of these approaches will depend on the issues being faced by policy-makers, and all the approaches have a contribution to make. In addition to the four main types of analysis identified, in certain cases it may be appropriate to undertake macro-economic evaluations. This is discussed further below but is only appropriate where a programme or investment is on such a large scale that it is likely to have macro-economic consequences.

Chart 1.1 is a schematic presentation of the applicability of and relationship between the alternative techniques. The chart shows that strategic reviews are most commonly applied to reviews of public policy or expenditure programmes and to the examination of public and private sector

CHART 1.1 APPLICABILITY AND RELATIONSHIPS BETWEEN TECHNIQUES			
Issues to be addressed	**What is relevant approach**	**Areas where most commonly applied**	**Key features and linkages**
Fundamental review of policies/ organisations/ expenditure programmes Need to question basic objectives/ rationale as well as effectiveness	**Strategic reviews**	Reviews of public policy/expenditure programmes Examination of public and private sector organisations	**Strategic reviews** Consideration of objectives/rationale for intervention — Cost-effectiveness
If there is agreement on basic operational objectives Need to focus only on efficiency/ effectiveness	**Cost-effectiveness reviews**	Evaluation of current expenditure programmes	**Cost-effectiveness reviews** Costs, efficiency, economy, effectiveness
Project expected to stand alone without continuing subsidy	**Financial appraisals**	Appraisal of commercial investments	**Financial appraisals** Projection of cash flows, treatment of risk, financial decision-making criteria
If benefits of project are not traded in market If economic distortions or externalities suggest that market prices would not reflect economic costs or benefits	**Economic cost/benefit appraisals**	Appraisal of public sector capital projects or private capital projects seeking EU or national government aid	**Cost-benefit appraisals** Projections of economic costs and benefits, treatment of risk, financial decision-making criteria
If project/ expenditure programme is so large that it would have macro-economic implications	**Macro-economic evaluations**	Evaluation of aggregate national expenditure programmes	**Macro-economic evaluations** Identification of macro-impacts, consideration of impact on projections, comparison of modified projections with initial projections

organisations. It is also suggested that strategic reviews encompass, among other things, a consideration of cost-effectiveness issues. In practice, however, detailed cost-effectiveness studies should only be applied to the evaluation of expenditure programmes where there is agreement on the basic operational objectives. Such evaluations are also likely to consider the operational aspects of efficiency and economy in more detail than would be undertaken as part of a general strategic review.

The chart also indicates that financial and economic cost-benefit appraisals are addressing similar issues, and both involve the projection of costs and benefits, the treatment of risk, and the generation of key decision-making criteria. The difference between these two approaches relates primarily to differences in the prices used. Cost-benefit studies are only applicable where market prices do not exist or where there are particular reasons why market prices are not appropriate.

To some extent a cost-effectiveness review could be seen as one aspect of a cost-benefit study, and in principle this is the case, as it will examine costs issues. In practice, however, cost-effectiveness studies require different skills and involve a much more detailed operational review than would usually be undertaken by economists in the context of economic cost-benefit appraisals. Cost-effectiveness studies are also most commonly used in the evaluation of current expenditure programmes, while cost-benefit studies are most frequently used in the evaluation of capital projects.

While some of the assumptions derived from macro-modelling of the economy might be of use in cost-benefit studies, it is not appropriate for most individual project or programme evaluators to undertake a simulation of the macro-economic consequences.

Strategic reviews represent an overall framework for analysis, and all public sector activities or EU interventions should be subject to occasional strategic reviews. They are probably the most potentially useful approach to improving the economic returns on EU or other public sector expenditure programmes. Strategic reviews are applicable to both current and capital expenditure programmes.

Cost-effectiveness studies are particularly useful in evaluating non-infrastructural expenditure programmes in such areas as

- human resources,
- health and education,
- industrial development, and
- tourism promotion.

This type of analysis requires a very detailed operational review and should be undertaken either before new initiatives are introduced or every few years for major expenditure programmes. Cost-effectiveness studies are essential where market prices are not operative, to act as a spur to effectiveness and efficiency.

Financial appraisals are required for all commercial projects and for all projects or programmes where continuing subsidies are not proposed.

Cost-benefit analysis may be applicable where individual capital projects are proposed in areas such as roads, railways, air and sea ports, tourism infrastructure, and industrial and energy investments. Cost-benefit analysis should only be used where a commercial appraisal is not possible or where public policy issues indicate that because of certain factors (for example distortions or externalities) the financial appraisal may be inappropriate.

Each of these four approaches is discussed in this chapter. In view of the relevance of cost-benefit analysis and the technical nature of this approach, it is considered in more detail later in the book.

In reviewing a public expenditure project or programme, two particular issues must be considered: deadweight and displacement impacts. Both deal with the important but difficult issue of what would have been the case if the programme had not been in operation. The deadweight concept refers to the likelihood that an outcome or benefit would have occurred without the project or programme. Resources spent on the programme would, to that extent, have been wasted. The displacement concept refers to the extent to which the project would cause other activities that might have contributed to achieving the desired benefits to be cancelled or reduced. Displacement also refers to negative side-effects of a programme that reduce other contributions to the achievement of the objective.

1.3 STRATEGIC REVIEWS

Need for Periodic Strategic Reviews

All public policy interventions, including all current and capital public expenditure programmes, should be subject to periodic strategic reviews. The purpose of strategic reviews of public expenditure is to examine the main objectives of the expenditure or investment and the options for achieving these objectives. The latter element of strategic reviews inevitably involves an examination of effectiveness.

Strategic reviews of public sector investments and programmes can provide the framework within which other techniques for evaluating individual projects or programmes can be undertaken. Strategic analysis is usually more important in considering a series of investments that form a programme rather than in individual project evaluations, although a strategic perspective can be useful in the latter context. The formulation of overall policies or programmes can often be more significant than the selection of individual investment projects. Strategic reviews are of most benefit in considering the key issue of the framing of policies.

Nature of Strategic Reviews

The nature of a strategic review will be directly determined by the area of expenditure under review, and, as a result, strategic reviews will differ significantly. Strategic reviews represent a broad approach to evaluations rather than the application of a specific technique.

A strategic review will inevitably evaluate the merits of the objectives. In a public policy context, objectives will usually be provided in broad terms by governments. These will often require more detailed formulation by government officials. A strategic review will in general consider the rationale for the public sector intervention as well as its effectiveness and will attempt in some way to relate the likely outcomes to the costs of the investment or programme expenditures.

In the case of economic policy, an analysis will be undertaken of what is usually referred to as the strategic threats and opportunities facing the sector of activity or the specific project. For social expenditure programmes such terms are usually not relevant, and other approaches to clarifying objectives and the consideration of alternative delivery mechanisms will usually be necessary.

Contrast with Private Sector Reviews

Strategic reviews in the private sector or in the commercial public sector are often different in focus and approach from those that can be usefully applied to evaluating EU or other public sector investment or current expenditure programmes. However, in certain cases techniques or approaches from private sector strategic reviews, such as the strategic business unit or portfolio planning matrices—which attempt to assist in dealing with such questions as the identification of the relevant market or business segment, the competition, and the competitive position—are sometimes applicable to strategic reviews in the more market-related areas of the public sector. The key issue of the rationale for public sector intervention must, however, always be addressed as part of strategic reviews of public policy. In many cases the form in which commercial strategic reviews are applied can be modified in evaluating effectiveness where output or services are not traded in the market. Also, some concepts that can assist in understanding the link between competitive strategy and industry structure, such as the industry structure model (see Porter, 1980), can be applied to the review of economic expenditure programmes in areas such as industrial development.

The techniques of strategic planning as used by the commercial sector can often be adapted to assist in answering some of the key questions essential to a strategic review of public sector programmes. The focus on issues such as sectoral structure and competitive position or industry analysis can also be very important in evaluating some areas of public sector expenditure. (For example, it is essential that such issues are evaluated as part of a strategic analysis of the effectiveness of EU or government expenditure on areas such as tourism marketing.) Some apparently sophisticated strategic planning techniques that have been used in the private sector may, however, have more packaging than substance and, while useful in sharpening the focus on certain areas, may lack the rigour necessary for evaluating public sector investments. Techniques surrounded by jargon must be assessed to ensure that they will assist in a disciplined assessment of the areas under review. In the author's experience the application of any specific strategic planning technique is rarely if ever sufficient for a comprehensive strategic review of a public sector investment programme, and a range of approaches is often required. An example of a strategic evaluation of a public sector tourism marketing programme is given in example 1.1.

Example 1.1   Evaluation of a Public Sector Current Expenditure Programme: a Tourism Marketing Example

OVERALL PROGRAMME EVALUATION

The tourism sector in Ireland plays an important role in the economy and is a major employer. In 1986 the Government decided to commission consultants to undertake a fundamental strategic review of tourism policy. The background to the review was the fact that despite the significance of tourism to the economy, Ireland had been losing its share of the international tourism market to its competitors. Tourism revenue in 1985 was below the 1979 level in real terms. Market share in Britain, the United States and Canada had declined, and Ireland had a very small and static market share in Germany and France. The decline of Ireland's market share in the United States and Britain alone had resulted in a loss of 637 million ECUs over the period 1975–85.

The strategic review identified three main reasons for the poor performance over the period. Firstly, the Irish tourism product, in range, standards, and facilities, was at that stage deficient compared with its competitors. Secondly, for important elements of the tourism product, Ireland was not at the time price-competitive. Thirdly, there had been major weaknesses in the marketing of tourism.

Of interest is the approach taken as part of the strategic review to the evaluation of the national tourism marketing programmes, and in particular the approach taken to evaluating the overseas distribution aspects of tourism marketing and secondly the evaluation of public expenditure on overseas tourism promotion.

APPROACH TO EVALUATING THE DISTRIBUTION OF TOURISM

The evaluation of the overseas distribution of tourism was approached by analysing the overall competitive strength or weakness of overseas distribution and by undertaking a trend analysis over a five-year period. This approach indicated that the distribution of Irish tourism with overseas tour operators was very weak and had not been increasing, except in the United States. For example, the research showed that in the important German market the number of tour operators offering holidays in Ireland fell from 79 in 1980 to 52 in 1985. It also showed that distribution in Britain and France was static over the same period and that there was a very high turnover among the tour operators offering holidays in Ireland in the period 1980–86, reflecting dissatisfaction with product quality and profitability prospects.

INNOVATIVE TECHNIQUES FOR EVALUATING PROMOTIONAL EXPENDITURES

The analysis of public expenditure on overseas marketing involved a detailed examination of the costs per holidaymaker of destination advertising. The findings suggested that the public sector expenditure on marketing was very costly, reflecting the high cost per holidaymaker of destination advertising for small countries such as Ireland. The analysis of the costs compared with likely estimates of revenue generated indicated the need for a reallocation of resources. One of the techniques used to evaluate the public expenditure on overseas marketing was the use of survey research on whether holidaymakers had seriously considered other locations, and to combine this research with tourism marketing expenditure data and with separate information on holidaymakers' spending. This analysis indicated that the marketing costs per non-committed holidaymaker—those who seriously considered countries other than Ireland as a destination—were unacceptably high when compared with estimated revenue generated. For example, the marketing cost per non-committed British holidaymaker was nearly 161 ECU, while average expenditure of British visitors to Ireland was about 185 ECU, excluding fares. The situation in North America was somewhat better, with an expenditure per non-committed holidaymaker of 193 ECU against an average spending of 495 ECU. In Continental Europe the situation was significantly worse, with marketing costs as a proportion of revenue generated being 106 per cent.

METHODOLOGICAL POINTS

A number of interesting methodological points are evident from this case study: firstly, the fact that expenditure on what is generally perceived as an appropriate area such as marketing does not imply that the expenditure is cost-effective, and secondly, the importance of developing innovative techniques for evaluating expenditure, often combining data from different sources and from different approaches. The example above also highlighted the importance of micro-measurements of effectiveness and rejected as misleading the use of regression analysis, which showed a correlation between tourism promotional budgets and holidaymakers' expenditure data.

Source: Price Waterhouse (1987).

Elements of a Strategic Review

Strategic reviews of public sector policies or investments are usually complex and involve a judgment of both external and internal factors relevant to the area of public expenditure. Because of their complexity, the nature of such reviews will vary significantly, and they are therefore not amenable to a specific technique. Effective strategic reviews require both rigorous analysis and creativity of ideas. Often creativity will also be required in designing methods to use as part of a specific strategic review as well as in the subsequent development of strategy. All strategic reviews must be concerned with questioning the objectives or purpose of the expenditure or investment, and once these are agreed the focus should be on the ability to achieve the objectives and the most cost-effective approach possible. While it is not possible to design a standard technique or method for a strategic review of public sector investments or programmes, some of the typical elements of such a review are presented in chart 1.2.

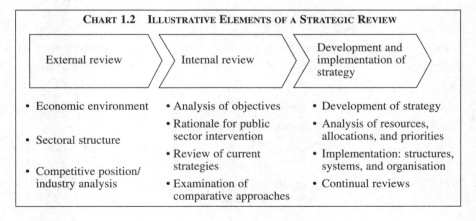

CHART 1.2   ILLUSTRATIVE ELEMENTS OF A STRATEGIC REVIEW

External review	Internal review	Development and implementation of strategy
• Economic environment	• Analysis of objectives	• Development of strategy
• Sectoral structure	• Rationale for public sector intervention	• Analysis of resources, allocations, and priorities
• Competitive position/ industry analysis	• Review of current strategies	• Implementation: structures, systems, and organisation
	• Examination of comparative approaches	• Continual reviews

External Review

It is essential in a strategic review of public sector investments to undertake a detailed analysis in order to develop a coherent view of the short-term and long-term external environment. External reviews must go far beyond the mere collection of data about economic developments, the structure of the sector in which the investment or expenditure takes place, or the competitive position or industry analysis. Rapid changes in the external environment (for example arising from the integration of EU policies, the liberalisation of European capital markets, dramatic movements in exchange rates, and rapid shifts in technology and market prospects) have profound implications for the range of strategic alternatives facing policy-makers. A simple forecasting exercise based on past trends may be useful but is only the first step in what may be required as part of a detailed understanding of the external environment.

Internal Review

An analysis of internal factors relevant to the investment or expenditure programme is the core of a strategic review. This will involve an analysis of the objectives of the investment or programme. The specification of clear and consistent objectives for a public sector programme is essential and is usually much more difficult than with private sector investments, where the return on shareholders' funds is usually the key objective.

For public sector investment or expenditure programmes it is important to differentiate between primary objectives (such as a specific contribution to economic or social objectives) and secondary objectives (such as quality of services to a client group). It is essential to map out the required performance or objectives before a strategic review can be effectively undertaken. Investment or other public sector expenditure programmes must be designed within a strategic context consistent with the overall objectives.

Once the objectives have been evaluated, a key element of a strategic review is an examination of the current strategies in terms of their effectiveness. The issue of cost-effectiveness is discussed in section 1.4 below, but, in summary, this will necessitate detailed empirical research. In practice the correct formulation of the information requirements and the development of approaches to obtaining this information often represent the most important tasks facing an analyst. This involves examining the past performance of the strategy in the achievement of its objectives. An analysis of performance indicators or performance measures, where available, will be required. Performance measures represent the yardsticks for monitoring or evaluating performance in terms of the achievement of objectives. Often, however, existing performance measures may be badly specified or non-existent. In such cases new primary sources of information may need to be created. In addition a gap analysis (a technique for comparing performance or targets against forecasts over a period) can in some cases be useful for monitoring and analysing the effectiveness of the underlying strategy.

It is essential in reviewing current strategies to understand the determinants of the outcomes of the strategy, as there can be no effective strategic review without an understanding of the forces at work. This is particularly important since the alleged outcome of a public expenditure programme may be due to other factors, such as a favourable international economic environment. Simple statistical correlations between expenditure on a specific programme or investment and a macro-outcome may often simply reflect spurious correlations. (See example 1.1.)

An interview programme with the key policy-makers in the member-state or in the European Commission, as appropriate, will be required as part of the review of current strategies. It is essential that structured interviews be undertaken, as these can often save significant time in identifying key areas for further analysis. Structured interviews should be designed with a formal agenda, and the analyst should identify in advance the precise information required and the areas to be discussed. The interviews should also allow scope for discussion on other areas that were not previously identified but that may be relevant to the evaluation.

The comparison of the 'with' and 'without' public sector investment scenario is frequently one of the most difficult practical tasks in strategic reviews and usually requires the development of micro-measures of effectiveness. Also essential in the internal review element of a strategic analysis is the examination of comparative approaches or strategies designed to achieve the same objective. An examination of international experience can often be of great benefit in this task.

The final issue that must be part of a strategic review is an analysis of the rationale for the intervention arising from factors such as market failure or externalities. (This is discussed in more detail in the review of cost-benefit analysis in chapter 3.)

Development and Implementation of Strategy

On the basis of the analysis of the external environment and the detailed 'internal' review, the key task is usually to develop or evaluate an appropriate strategy for the investment or expenditure programme. This may, of course, involve deciding that no investment or programme is required. Assuming, however, that the investment or programme is appropriate, the development of the strategic direction for the programme can be the most important task in ensuring effectiveness and consistency with other elements of EU or government policies.

An analysis of the appropriate allocation of resources and priorities within the programme is necessary. Unless this is specified, confusion can arise later about whether the strategy is being implemented. The implementation issue is of fundamental importance, as strategy and execution must be inextricably linked. This will involve deciding not only on resource priorities but on structures, systems, and organisational options.

At the stage of the formulation of a strategic plan this should also include a monitoring process involving continual reviews of the investment or programme.

Despite the absence of any specific 'off-the-shelf' technique or method for undertaking strategic reviews, and the complexity of such reviews, they are of fundamental importance in deciding on future policy directions. The analysis of specific EU or other public sector investments considered in detail in this book must be considered within the strategic context for the investment. Apart from the appraisal of specific capital investments, strategic reviews are, in the author's opinion, probably the most important approach available to assist in improving the economic returns of programmes funded by the public sector.

1.4 COST-EFFECTIVENESS STUDIES

Cost-effectiveness is an important aspect of the evaluation of public sector investments and is particularly useful in the appraisal of non-infrastructural expenditure programmes. This is essentially an analysis that compares the cost of providing the same benefit in different ways in order to establish the cheapest way of achieving an objective and of considering whether the investment or programme is effective in meeting its objectives. It does not attempt to measure in a quantified manner whether the economic benefits exceed the costs involved. Cost-effectiveness analysis is, however, useful where there has been a policy decision to provide some activity, such as defence or a health service investment. It is also useful where an investment will jointly benefit many people and where it is difficult to exclude potential users from the benefit. In some of these cases the benefits cannot be easily valued in monetary terms, but it is important to consider the cost-effectiveness of the particular investments or programmes. Once a decision is made to proceed with an investment or government programme, ensuring that it is delivered in the most cost-effective way is of great importance.

Various terms are used to describe cost-effectiveness analysis in different EU countries, and in Britain the focus has been on what is described as 'value-for-money auditing'. In essence this looks at the objectives of a programme or investment and considers whether it has been effective in achieving the objectives. In some cases the application of this technique has been reduced to the use of a formula that relates costs to a specific quantified benefit of an investment. The cost-effectiveness study often confronts the difficulty (central also to cost-benefit analysis) of quantifying the various outputs or benefits. To see if a programme is cost-effective, it will often be necessary to come up with detailed measures of what it is trying to achieve. But, unlike cost-benefit analysis, the cost-effectiveness study will not need to go the further step of putting a monetary value on these achievements. The increasing presentation of EU structural funds on a programme basis and the use of programme budgeting in a number of countries may facilitate a comparison of alternative means of achieving the same objective. Sensibly applied, this technique can provide a very useful, pragmatic way of measuring the effectiveness of structural funds or other public sector investments. While cost-effectiveness analysis is more limited in evaluative scope than some other approaches, it does enable an evaluation to be undertaken of non-financial inputs and outputs. The key in this area, as in so many other aspects of project or programme evaluation, is the judgment of the evaluators.

Cost-Effectiveness and the Three Es

Cost-effectiveness techniques are sometimes referred to as ways of evaluating performance as measured by the 'three Es', namely economy, efficiency and effectiveness in the use of resources. Economy in this context usually refers to ensuring that resources are secured in the lowest-cost manner. The related concept of efficiency refers to the use of resources to obtain the maximum output for any resources used. In many instances, for practical purposes economy and efficiency (which both relate ultimately to the quality of the operational management of the investment or programme) can be considered simultaneously. Effectiveness is concerned with the extent to which an investment or programme achieves its objectives.

Often cost-effectiveness studies have been inappropriately confined by management consultants, trained in an audit tradition, to focusing on the economy and efficiency aspects rather than the issue of effectiveness, which is usually more difficult to evaluate. This is not to suggest that efficiency in the management of inputs and activities is unimportant. In public sector

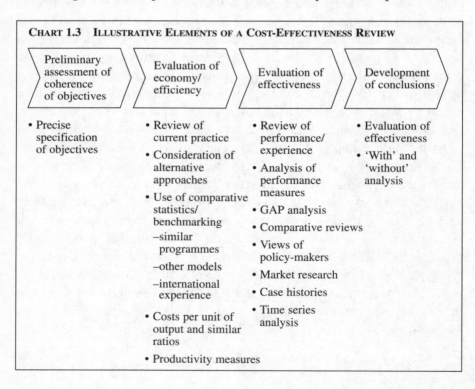

CHART 1.3   ILLUSTRATIVE ELEMENTS OF A COST-EFFECTIVENESS REVIEW

Preliminary assessment of coherence of objectives	Evaluation of economy/ efficiency	Evaluation of effectiveness	Development of conclusions
• Precise specification of objectives	• Review of current practice • Consideration of alternative approaches • Use of comparative statistics/ benchmarking –similar programmes –other models –international experience • Costs per unit of output and similar ratios • Productivity measures	• Review of performance/ experience • Analysis of performance measures • GAP analysis • Comparative reviews • Views of policy-makers • Market research • Case histories • Time series analysis	• Evaluation of effectiveness • 'With' and 'without' analysis

programmes, where market pressures are not available to act as a spur to efficiency, the way in which resources are managed requires continuous review. One aspect of this that is particularly important and is considered in chapter 7 relates to the control of capital costs. Despite the importance of economy and efficiency, effectiveness is often the most important issue requiring evaluation in the context of EU structural funds or other public sector expenditure programmes. If the rationale of the programme is flawed, intensifying the programme as a result of securing internal efficiencies may be largely irrelevant.

The evaluation of the cost-effectiveness of public sector investments or programmes cannot be carried out using a standard approach, because of the diversity of such programmes and activities. The evaluation methods must therefore be tailored to the specific investment or programme under review. Some of the typical elements of cost-effectiveness reviews are, however, presented in chart 1.3.

Preliminary Assessment of Coherence of Objectives

The evaluation of effectiveness arising from some investment or expenditure programme requires that objectives be specified precisely. Of course, questioning the relevance of the basic objectives is more a task for a strategic review than for a cost-effectiveness exercise. Nevertheless, some brief assessment of the coherence of objectives is a necessary preliminary here too. It is also important to note that sometimes a project may start out as a cost-effectiveness exercise but it soon transpires that what is really required is an overall strategic policy evaluation of a programme or investment. This should involve questioning the underlying rationale of the objectives and whether they are appropriate in the light of current economic factors or current policy developments.

Evaluation of Economy and Efficiency

Ways of improving effectiveness with fewer resources can be very important, particularly in the evaluation of current expenditure programmes where there is a consensus on the merits of the overall programme.

This will involve a review of current practice and also consideration of alternative approaches to achieving the same output or benefit. This may require an examination of best practice, either nationally or internationally.

The choice of models for comparison requires case-by-case consideration, and the judgment and experience of the analyst is essential. There is always a danger that inappropriate models will be chosen, because of the ease of assembling information (perhaps in a neighbouring country), rather than by identifying best practice or the most appropriate model for comparison. Choosing the appropriate model often requires specialist sectoral knowledge and experience of international developments in the area under review. It also requires an ability to seek out and interpret information. This will usually require wide experience rather than any specific analytical skills.

The use of comparative statistics to assist in analysing the efficiency and effectiveness of public sector investments or programmes is very similar to the technique of 'benchmarking' that is widely used in the commercial sector to measure aspects of efficiency. While such comparisons in isolation are unlikely to be conclusive, they often provide a guide to areas that merit further examination.

In practice, obtaining reliable and relevant performance measures as well as comparative statistics can be the basis on which a cost-effectiveness study will stand or fall. The employment of a wide range of sophisticated market research techniques as well as 'bottom-up modelling' exercises may also be required.

Also relevant in examining the efficiency of an investment or programme is the development and analysis of cost indicators, for example the use of costs per unit of output or similar ratios. If these are correctly designed they can be a powerful and widely understood measure of efficiency. The use of the related technique of productivity measures or indicators can also be of benefit.

Evaluation of Effectiveness

For many areas of EU or other public sector programmes the fundamental question is their effectiveness. This will involve a detailed review of performance and experience.

Some of the elements in evaluating effectiveness were outlined in the discussion of strategic reviews referred to above. This included the use of gap analysis and the analysis of performance indicators or performance measures. Analysing or developing key performance measures is an important task in cost-effectiveness studies. In the author's opinion there is a danger that performance measures will mainly be seen as measures of activity rather than of the impact of the activity. In considering performance measures it is necessary to ask whether they are appropriate for the measuring of effectiveness and also whether reliable data is available or can be generated.

In the discussion of strategic reviews, reference was made to examining comparative approaches or strategies designed to achieve the same objectives. Also relevant in the context of cost-effectiveness examinations is the use of comparative reviews of similar approaches or strategies in other parts of the member-state or in other countries. This can involve the examination of comparative statistics for similar programmes or investments or, in certain cases, comparisons from apparently unrelated sectors or programmes, although clearly this will be applicable only in selected cases. Such comparative reviews are of most value in designing future programmes or investments rather than in subsequent evaluation, although they can sometimes be of use in that task. An interview programme with key policy-makers (as was suggested for strategic reviews) will also usually be required.

One of the most useful elements in evaluating effectiveness is the use of market research. This is particularly valuable in measuring the impact of an investment or programme on assumed beneficiaries. It will usually involve industry or sector research and not simply consumer research, although some adaptations of the latter can be of benefit. In considering market research it is essential to decide in advance on the key areas for research. The specification of the issues to be examined and, where relevant, the design of the research questionnaire can be of critical importance. Too often research questionnaires, or the specification of the issues to be reviewed as part of an interview programme, have been inadequately framed, as a result of a lack of understanding of the key issues required as part of an evaluation.

The use of a pilot survey is often desirable, particularly where the issues concerned are complex or where there are concerns over the interpretation of survey questions or the availability of information requirements that are specified in a particular manner.

It is also important to consider the approach to the research, including the research method and the sample design. The representativeness and/or reliability of market research findings can be evaluated by comparing the findings with data from more comprehensive sources (for example national census data). The effective implementation of the survey and the analysis of the results are also of key importance and will require the use of experienced analysts.

Detailed case histories involving the monitoring of the experience of beneficiaries of the programme or investment can also be of use. In addition, time series analysis of relevant outputs of the investment can be used to effect. In analysing time series data it is important, if use is made of monthly or quarterly data, to consider the relevant seasonal factors. It may also be appropriate to adjust time series for cyclical patterns or for irregular or outliner observations. In estimating the trend in time series data it may be appropriate to consider a number of formal statistical methods.

Development of Conclusions

The development of conclusions and, where appropriate, recommendations is of course the reason for undertaking cost-effectiveness studies. These should be based on the analysis of efficiencies but should also take account of the primary issue of effectiveness.

In designing cost-effectiveness approaches it is essential to consider the extent to which outputs of the investment or programme were related to that activity or to some other external factor. The 'with' and 'without' issue was referred to in the discussion of strategic reviews. While the disentangling of alternative determinants with precision may not always, or indeed even usually, be possible, the absence of consideration of this issue is one of the main deficiencies of many cost-effectiveness assignments.

As suggested in this discussion, cost-effectiveness studies can overlap with strategic reviews, and the coherence of objectives as well as the best ways to achieve a given objective can be questioned. In general, however, cost-effectiveness analysis is used where there is policy agreement on the merits of achieving an objective, and the task then is how to achieve the objective in the most effective way—in other words, in a way that minimises the costs involved. This approach is particularly useful where it is difficult or impossible to assign specific monetary values to the achievement of an objective. The task of comparing alternative approaches in order to determine the best way to attain a specific objective is frequently the key issue facing policy-makers. Cost-effectiveness studies are therefore a potentially useful approach to the evaluation of public sector programmes or investments.

1.5 FINANCIAL APPRAISALS

The commercial or financial viability of an investment is of critical importance in project appraisals where continuing subsidy is not envisaged. There are two important aspects of financial appraisals: the cash flow projections, and the financial return on the project. Even projects that are expected to record a positive financial return must ensure that the cash flow is sufficient to ensure their viability. This is of particular importance in the first few years of operation. Many of the techniques involved in financial appraisals are common to economic appraisals, and are discussed in chapter 2. As this study is concerned with the economic evaluation of investments and programmes, the issues involved in financial appraisals are not considered in detail. This is not to underestimate the critical importance of financial viability for many projects.

1.6 COST-BENEFIT ANALYSIS

There are important limitations to cost-benefit techniques. If sensibly applied, however, they represent a very useful approach to the economic evaluation of individual capital investments. For that reason these techniques are considered in further detail in this book.

Cost-benefit analysis attempts to measure in monetary terms the discounted values of all the costs and benefits over the life of a project, on the basis that only those projects where the benefits exceed the costs should be undertaken. This is necessary in order to maximise net benefits. Given a range of alternative possible projects, any specific investment should only be undertaken if the benefits exceed those of the next-best alternative course of action. The foundations for cost-benefit analysis are in welfare economics, which is concerned with the efficient allocation of scarce resources. This is considered in more detail in chapter 3.

There are three main tasks involved in cost-benefit analysis. Firstly there is the monetary valuation of different costs and benefits, which will involve the use of opportunity costs. The use of shadow prices or opportunity costs is only appropriate where market prices do not adequately measure economic costs or benefits, because of economic distortions or externalities. Where such circumstances do not exist there is no need for a cost-benefit appraisal. These areas are examined in chapter 4. The second task involves the relative valuation of costs and benefits occurring at different times, which is dealt with in chapter 5; and the final element involves the treatment of risks, which is discussed in chapter 6. The issue of the relative valuation of costs and benefits occurring at different times and the treatment of risks also applies to financial appraisals.

Cost-benefit analysis has been successfully applied to numerous areas of EU and other public sector investments. The initial widespread application of the techniques was in the areas of transport and water resources, but its application has grown enormously to include the key public expenditure areas of health and education as well as energy investments, tourism, and industrial development.

1.7 MACRO-ECONOMIC EVALUATIONS

In addition to the four main types of analysis discussed above, one additional approach to the evaluation of a series of public sector investments is the attempt to evaluate their macro-economic impact. This can be achieved by the use of a macro-model of the economy of the country. This approach makes possible a formal quantified assessment of the potential effects of the investment programme. The evaluation of macro-economic impacts will almost inevitably require the use of a formal macro-economic model of the economy, supported by other models. This may facilitate the quantification of the long-term implications of the investments; this is achieved by comparing the projected performance of the economy as a result of the investments under review with benchmark projections without the investments.

Benefits and Limitations of Macro-Economic Evaluations

It is essential to understand the benefits and limitations of a macro-economic impact approach to the evaluation of an investment programme. The main benefit arises from a formal quantification of the potential macro-economic impact of the investments based on certain assumptions. This has an advantage over considering individual investments in isolation if it would be incorrect to assume that the economy-wide impact will be the simple aggregation of the individual project benefits. Such an approach does not, however, provide a detailed micro-economic study of the costs and benefits of different projects. It may be useful in certain situations in considering the long-term impact in broad terms but does not accommodate the level of detail of relevance to individual project appraisals. The effects of an investment programme on demand can be relatively easily accommodated by macro-economic modelling, but the measurement of critical supply-side effects are more difficult to handle.

Macro-economic models take account of a variety of effects on the economy. The modelling of the short-term or demand-side effects of an investment programme are well understood, and such impacts as the generation of economic activity in the construction sector will represent the principal short-term impact of a large-scale investment programme before the investment takes place. A comprehensive examination of the macro-economic impact of the demand implications can be undertaken by such an approach. The supply-side implications of investments will take longer to produce an impact. but these benefits are usually the rationale for the investments and represent the return on the expenditure. The nature of the macro-economic modelling system used will determine the extent to which the supply-side impacts can be handled but in general will require additional information that can only be provided by more micro-studies. Depending on the specific model used, it may be possible for some sectoral results to be formally incorporated in the specifications of the model, while others may be simulated separately.

The benefits and constraints of formal macro-economic modelling of investments can be seen by considering the evaluation of infrastructural investments, for example expenditure on roads or railways. The impact of these investments on increased demand arising from their construction can be estimated, but for the critical supply-side impact the model will depend on external inputs that can only be obtained from the results of individual project evaluations. (Individual project evaluation results may also be misleading if they do not take account of the wider impact of the investment.) The macro-economic evaluation is therefore dependent on the results of micro-studies or is forced to make assumptions on the rate of return in the investment programme. The impact of the supply-side effects can be considered by examining the output of the macro-modelling exercises with and without the supply-side effects, or alternatively by considering the impact of modelling a range of alternative rates of return. Macro-economic evaluations of public sector programmes are only of use in special cases, where a programme or investment is of such a large scale that it is likely to have macro-economic implications. In considering the use of this approach, the difficulties in accurate modelling of national economies must also be recognised.

*   *   *

In considering the overall approaches to evaluation, it is suggested that all sizable projects that are funded by the EU or by national exchequers should be subject to detailed appraisal and evaluation. It is usually appropriate to undertake a preliminary appraisal of proposals, and only those that appear sensible at this stage should be subject to a detailed evaluation. It is also important that post-project appraisals are undertaken, in order to improve the procedures and methods of evaluation.

2

TECHNIQUES FOR INVESTMENT APPRAISAL

It is useful to review the techniques that are available for determining the return on investments. These techniques provide the basis for decisions on the merits of individual investments. They are applicable both to financial appraisals and to cost-benefit evaluations.

Three main techniques are used to measure the return on investments:

- Net present value
- Internal rate of return
- Pay-back

2.1 NET PRESENT VALUE

One of the most important methods or techniques for the evaluation of investment projects is that of net present value (NPV). This approach can be defined as follows:

$$\text{NPV} = x_0 + \frac{x_1}{1+r} + \frac{x_2}{(1+r)^2} + \dots + \frac{x_N}{(1+r)^N} = \sum_{n=1}^{N} \frac{x_n}{(1+r)^n}$$

where NPV = net present value, x is the net benefit flow from the project, r is the interest or discount rate, each year is indicated by n, and the terminal date is N. This technique enables one to add up all the benefits (revenues) of an investment and subtract the costs. Both the benefits and the costs are discounted back to the specified time period in order to give the present value of the net benefits of the investment. (The issue of discounting is discussed in more detail in chapter 5.) The time is usually measured from the present but could be measured from the year in which the project will start.

In choosing between projects or in deciding whether to proceed with a

25

specific investment proposal, the NPV technique is the best way of evaluating the investment. In NPV calculations the interest or discount rate to be used for the test is selected in advance so that projects are recommended if the NPV discounted at a certain rate is positive, assuming that alternative projects do not have a higher return. The NPV technique, in summary, translates the estimated future net benefits of an investment in value terms to the valuation in terms of an earlier period. It thus represents the capitalised values of a stream of net benefits. This involves discounting and aggregating future costs and benefits. In financial appraisals of investments this technique is usually referred to as discounted cash flow (DCF) analysis where monetary revenues and costs are discounted. A positive discounted NPV result in financial appraisals indicates that a project is financially viable.

2.2 INTERNAL RATE OF RETURN

An often-used summary indicator of the return on a project is the internal rate of return (IRR). This is closely related to the NPV technique, and is defined as the discount rate at which the net present value of a project is equal to 0. In other words, the IRR is the rate (r^*) that equates the net present value of a project to 0. This is illustrated as follows:

$$\text{NPV} = 0 = x_0 + \frac{x_1}{1 + r^*} + \ldots + \frac{x_N}{(1 + r^*)^N}$$

where x is the net benefit after subtracting costs, and r^*= IRR. In such circumstances this is the same formula as used for NPV calculations, but the discount rate r^* is set so that the NPV estimate is equated to 0. The IRR is therefore the solution rate of interest that equates to 0 the NPV of the discounted cash flows of an investment.

The internal rate of return is sometimes used as a decision rule whereby a project is approved if the internal rate of return (r^*) is equal to or greater than the agreed discount or interest rate.

When compared with a test rate, the internal rate of return seems to be a convenient way of summarising the merits of a project. In fact it usually makes no difference whether one uses IRR or NPV to rank projects; but in the cases where it does make a difference, the IRR always gives a ranking that is demonstrably wrong. Furthermore, some projects have more than one IRR, so it is not clear which one to choose. All in all, NPV is a more reliable indicator.

There are two main situations where IRR gives the wrong answer. The first arises where two mutually exclusive projects are being considered. For example, we might be faced with a situation where two projects are competing for a particular location. The weakness of IRR in this situation is due to its emphasis on rate of return rather than on size of return. It might, in such circumstances, be wise to discard a small-scale project with a high rate of return in favour of a much larger project that, though it has a lower rate of return, nevertheless yields much higher total net benefits. If we must choose between a 1 billion ECU project yielding 7 per cent and a 1 million ECU project yielding 8 per cent, then the larger project must be preferred.

The other situation where IRR gives the wrong answer arises where the time pattern of net benefit flows from the project is such as to make the project less advantageous for lower rates of discount. This crops up most often when there are heavy expenditures late in the life of the project, such as may happen with environmental clean-up costs. The IRR of such a project is a discount rate at which the project will break even, but at any lower discount rates the same project may be disadvantageous. (See example 2.1.) The problem of more than one IRR can arise where a project receives net benefits in one year and incurs additional costs in a later year or years. In other words, this problem occurs when positive cash flows are followed by negative cash flows. If there are multiple changes between negative and positive cash flows, multiple IRR estimates can result.

Despite the fact that the IRR is widely used and usually gives the right result, its imperfections mean that it is not appropriate as the decision criterion for projects.

Example 2.1 Weakness of Pay-back and IRR Techniques

The annual flow of revenue for three projects is shown, each of them involving an initial outlay of 1 million ECU. Project A pays back quickly (four-year pay-back period if undiscounted, five years if discounted at 5 per cent) but has a short lifetime. Project B pays back more slowly (five-year pay-back period undiscounted) but continues to provide net revenue for many years. Clearly it would be a mistake to select project A over project B because of its shorter pay-back period.

Project C illustrates some of the pitfalls that may be encountered by the user of IRR. This project is the same as project B except that there is a large negative flow in the last period, perhaps reflecting environmental clean-up obligations. In fact project C has two IRRs, at 9.68 and 12.75 per cent. Given a test discount rate of 5 per cent, the naïve analyst might be inclined to recommend proceeding with project C on this basis. In fact the NPV of project C is negative for any discount rate below 9.68 per cent. What is happening here is that a low discount rate implies that relatively greater attention must be paid to distant events, such as the clean-up cost. Depositing the 1 million ECU at 5 per cent will be a better strategy than investing it in project C, given the clean-up costs that would be faced in twenty years.

ANNUAL CASH FLOWS FOR THREE PROJECTS			
Year	A	B	C
0	−1.00	−1.00	−1.00
1	0.25	0.20	0.20
2	0.25	0.20	0.20
3	0.25	0.20	0.20
4	0.25	0.20	0.20
5	0.25	0.20	0.20
6		0.20	0.20
7		0.20	0.20
8		0.20	0.20
9		0.20	0.20
10		0.20	0.20
11		0.20	0.20
12		0.20	0.20
13		0.20	0.20
14		0.20	0.20
15		0.20	0.20

ANNUAL CASH FLOWS FOR THREE PROJECTS – CONTINUED			
Year	A	B	C
16		0.20	0.20
17		0.20	0.20
18		0.20	0.20
19		0.20	0.20
20			−4.50
Pay-back	4	5	5
Pay-back (discounted)	5	6	6
NPV at 5 per cent	0.08	1.42	−0.28
IRR	8.0	19.3	12.8;9.7

2.3 PAY-BACK

The pay-back period as a decision rule for investment appraisal is widely used in the private sector. The pay-back technique simply considers the number of years it is expected to take before the net income or net benefit from the investment pays back the initial investment—in other words, the number of years before the cost of the investment is recovered. Given the uncertainty regarding future revenues from investment expenditures beyond a certain period, it is sometimes argued that this technique is a useful and simple way of appraising investments. The alleged advantages of the technique relate to its simplicity and its use in highlighting the risks in a project.

There are, however, a number of serious problems in using this technique, which suggest that it is not appropriate on its own as an investment appraisal criterion. The limitations on the value of the technique relate in part to the fact that it does not take account of the timing of costs or benefits. This problem could be somewhat alleviated if the pay-back period technique were applied to discounted costs and benefits, but this would not take account of the fundamental deficiency that it does not take account of costs or benefits beyond the pay-back period.

This technique therefore would bias investment decisions in favour of investment expenditures with short-term rather than long-term benefits. This would seem particularly inappropriate for investments financed by EU structural funds, in view of the long-term sustainable economic development rationale that is the stated justification for these funds. The weakness inherent in the technique, which ignores costs and benefits beyond the pay-back period, is evident if one considers a comparison of two projects with very different estimated lifetime scales. The pay-back technique would, for example, suggest that a project with a pay-back period of four years is superior to one with a pay-back period of five years. If, however, the first project was at the end of its life after five years while the second project provided annual benefits for another fifteen years, the weakness of ignoring benefits after the pay-back period is clear. This is illustrated in example 2.1.

2.4 EVALUATION OF ALTERNATIVE TECHNIQUES

The analysis presented above suggests that the appropriate technique to use in the appraisal of investment expenditures is the discounted net present value approach. While the IRR and pay-back period are often used, they represent short-cuts that are not appropriate as investment appraisal criteria, given the availability of computer-based methods of calculation.

3

COST-BENEFIT ANALYSIS

3.1 OVERVIEW AND APPLICATION OF COST-BENEFIT ANALYSIS

Cost-benefit analysis (CBA) attempts to measure in monetary terms the discounted values of all the costs and benefits of an investment over the expected life of a project. This approach can also be used to evaluate policy decisions or current expenditure decisions rather than specific investments, although it is in relation to investment that it is more commonly used. In practice, attempting to provide precise estimates of the rate of return on current social and other expenditures is likely to be very difficult. This approach tackles the fundamental question of whether an investment should or should not be undertaken. Only projects where at a minimum the benefits exceed the costs should proceed. The approach considers an investment from the perspective of net social advantage or disadvantage. Indirect or spin-off costs and benefits are included in the calculation, as well as those directly connected with the project.

This approach is therefore the method by which the balance of advantages and disadvantages, or benefits and costs, is aggregated. It is concerned with evaluating the impact of an investment on the economy and thereby on the welfare of society.

Similarity to Financial Analysis

At one level the issues faced in applying cost-benefit analysis to the evaluation of public sector investments financed by structural funds or otherwise are the same as those facing companies or financial institutions in evaluating investments. Are the benefits from the investment sufficient to justify the costs and risks involved? Essentially this involves evaluating whether the sum of the benefits exceeds the total costs of the investment after discounting, i.e. after taking account of the time value of money. It is therefore not surprising that both cost-benefit and financial appraisals of investments have traditionally used the same decision-making techniques, such as NPV, IRR, and pay-back period, which were described in chapter 2.

Characteristics of Cost-Benefit Analysis

Given limited resources, a specific investment should only be undertaken if the benefits exceed those of the next-best alternative use of the resources. This is particularly relevant in evaluating the expenditure of EU structural funds.

As a cost-benefit appraisal of an investment is designed to consider the wider economic or social impact rather than the narrower financial impact, it differs from commercial financial appraisals. While the detailed methods of cost-benefit evaluations are very different from financial evaluations, it is important to recognise that the difference between the results is due to differences in the choice of prices and discount rates.

Cost-benefit analysis rather than financial analysis is only required when market prices are not available or are not adequate because of economic distortions or externalities. Market prices in general have a robustness and should be used unless there are clear reasons why they are not appropriate. In the absence of distortions the market prices will provide the best allocation of resources, apart from redistribution issues, which require other approaches. If there are economic distortions, then market prices may give the wrong signals for the allocation of investment funds. It should be realised that an investment may result in economic losses, even where a commercial evaluation may indicate profits, if prices are administratively determined. Example 3.1 illustrates the case of a government investment in the oil refining sector.

In considering the merits of an economic evaluation, it is essential to take account of the option of directly correcting for the distortion (through taxes, controls, etc.) rather than calculating cost-benefit valuations. This goes to the heart of public policy intervention, and it is necessary to recognise that if distortions exist, this may imply that the commercial sector is using the 'wrong' price signals. The possibility that the application of cost-benefit analysis using shadow prices for EU and exchequer-funded projects only may worsen the impact of the distortion should be recognised.

Example 3.1   Evaluation of a Public Sector Capital Investment: an Oil Refinery Example

In the early 1980s, through a combination of declining demand for oil products in western Europe and the previous completion of numerous refinery investments, excess capacity of basic distillation plant in the petroleum industry led to many refinery closures. The major international petroleum companies that jointly owned Ireland's only refinery (Whitegate in Cork Harbour) announced their decision to cease operations there, and offered the refinery for sale to the Government. The refinery was old and had limited flexibility in operation, but it was a major employer in an area where several other industrial plants had recently closed; furthermore, the issue of security of supply of petroleum to Ireland was raised. The Government decided to purchase the refinery and for a time to oblige all companies selling petroleum products in Ireland to purchase 35 per cent of their needs from the refinery. The price set for this mandatory purchase was related to the refinery's costs rather than international market prices.

A review group was established after about a year to evaluate the economic and other impacts of the refinery. According to media reports, the group concluded that, despite adequate financial performance, the true annual economic costs of operating the refinery were very high. The quoted estimates suggested that, based on an economic opportunity cost analysis, if the refinery had been operative throughout 1980 and 1981 this would imply economic losses of between $57 and $110 million for the two years taken together; this was of the order of 1 per cent of GDP. The main factor was the excessive price charged on the mandatory purchase, which added an amount equivalent to 37 ECU per household per annum to petroleum prices as well as contributing to higher electricity prices. It was also suggested that there was no evidence that the refinery had played any role in relation to security of supply in previous oil crises.

The example illustrates the importance of using the appropriate prices in an appraisal. If actual prices do not reflect true economic costs, they must not be used for the appraisal. In this case the deviation of the refinery's selling price from the true alternative cost of petroleum products was attributable to Government fiat. When valued at world market prices, the refinery was making a big loss. The example also highlights the importance of scepticism in assessing alleged strategic justifications for costly projects. As the economic impact was significantly influenced by international market conditions, this highlights the importance of careful consideration of demand projections, which are often very difficult in practice to get right.

Source: Tansey (1983) and other media reports.

Cost-benefit evaluations take account of costs and benefits accruing to individuals or groups in society that are not directly involved in the investment project. In simple terms, a cost-benefit appraisal of an investment involves aggregating all the discounted benefits to the wider community and subtracting all the discounted costs, regardless of whether these benefits or costs pass through the market mechanism. Costs and benefits are therefore also taken into account, even when they have no immediate market value.

The Concept of Shadow Pricing

At the core of cost-benefit evaluations of investments is the concept of opportunity costs or shadow pricing. Shadow prices are simply the specific estimated prices that are used in cost-benefit evaluations where it is assumed that market prices do not reflect economic costs or where no prices exist. As this is one of the aspects of cost-benefit analysis that is most difficult to explain and can sometimes appear to policy-makers to be very unrealistic and theoretical, it is considered in detail in chapter 4. To understand the rationale of this approach, its theoretical foundations are briefly discussed in section 3.2.

Social or opportunity costs attempt to measure the alternative social or economic value of resources. They apply to items that have a market value as well as to goods or services that are not traded in the market. Not all social or opportunity costs differ from market values, but in circumstances where unemployment and uncompetitive market practices exist, a divergence between market prices and social or opportunity costs or values may emerge.

In using shadow or imputed prices in cost-benefit appraisals, the focus should be on attempting to estimate how much consumers would pay for benefits if it was possible to charge for the benefits through a competitive market system. The task is therefore to estimate what value would be placed by consumers on the benefits and the resource costs involved. This is usually undertaken by inferring values from revealed market behaviour, although other methods are also used.

The adjustment of market prices to reflect wider social costs requires the use of shadow prices or social valuations. Correcting market prices by the use of shadow prices is, in practice, fraught with difficulties and is the main area where the evaluation of public sector investments is much more difficult than simply considering the commercial viability of an investment proposal. In commercial or financial investment appraisals, costs and benefits are automatically valued by market prices. The so-called invisible hand of the market provides an elaborate system of price signals that guides investment decisions. For public sector projects where distortions or externalities exist, financial appraisals may not be adequate for measuring the economic impact of a proposed investment.

Cost-benefit appraisals attempt to assign monetary values to all costs and benefits. Despite the best efforts of economists, however, some costs and benefits are intangible and are simply not amenable to monetary quantification, although with sensible application the range of intangible or non-measurable costs and benefits can be significantly reduced. In cases, however, where benefits or costs cannot be reasonably quantified in monetary terms it is important at least to identify and present these factors, which can then be explicitly considered by policy-makers. Despite the difficulties in accurately estimating shadow prices, this problem is somewhat reduced if consistency is applied in investment appraisals. A consistent framework for selecting individual projects can be as important in improving economic efficiency as any specific method of appraisal.

Multiplier Impact

The direct benefits of a project may underestimate the total impact due to the multiplier effect of the investment. In so far as the investment expenditure generates additional output and income it will circulate to other parts of the economy. An important issue sometimes ignored in project appraisals—

resulting in an overestimation of the multiplier impact—is the role of demand or other factors in influencing the productive capacity of the economy. This will in part depend on whether the additional expenditures generated are for services or manufactured goods. Increasingly with the internationalisation of EU economies, expenditure on manufactured goods may be reflected in an increase in imports. It is also important to consider capacity constraints and the impact of demand on price determination.

Any evaluation of the size of the multiplier impact must make assumptions regarding the marginal propensities to consume and save and the marginal propensity to import. The latter factor will be more significant in the smaller EU member-states.

In practical cases the analyst is faced with the decision whether to include an estimate of the multiplier effects on benefits in evaluating investment decisions. The arguments against including a multiplier impact tend to relate to practical concerns that benefits may be overestimated, leading to inappropriate investment decisions. This, however, does not justify excluding the multiplier impact but instead suggests that caution should be exercised in estimating its size.

Estimates of the overall size of the multiplier impact must be applied only to benefits where income or expenditure is involved and not to non-monetary benefits, even though these would be included in the cost-benefit calculation. Estimation of the multiplier impact must also take account of the lost multiplier effect arising from the potential use of the expenditure in some alternative use. This would suggest that the multiplier should be applied to the net expenditure impact of the output of the investment after taking account of the costs incurred.

It could be argued that the issue of whether to include a multiplier effect does not matter, in that cost-benefit evaluations of investments are attempting to evaluate the returns to the economy of alternative investments and that all that is required is for a consistent approach to be used. While this has much validity, the size of the multiplier may vary by project, depending on the significance of expenditures and non-monetary benefits as well as other specific project differences. Also of importance is the fact that an appraisal may be restricted to considering simply whether the economic benefits exceed the costs of the investment rather than a comparison of an infinite number of alternative projects. For this and other reasons it is suggested that a multiplier impact be included where feasible, although it is essential that the danger of overestimation of the size of the multiplier is realised. Not including a multiplier impact is usually of minor importance. There is, however, a need for consistency in the approach to the estimation of the size of the multiplier. In practice if a multiplier is needed it can probably be obtained from previous macro-economic modelling. Despite the attention sometimes given in individual project appraisals to the multiplier effect, most of the time its significance is likely to be small, as one is deciding between different uses of available funds.

System-wide Impact of Projects

Before the theoretical formulations for cost-benefit appraisals are briefly discussed, it is useful to consider the issue referred to in chapter 1 concerning whether individual project evaluations could be misleading if they do not take account of the wider impact of the investment. Two aspects of this question merit consideration. First is the choice of options; this is considered further in chapter 8, as investment project appraisals must implicitly make decisions on the range of options for consideration. The second issue relates to the fact that a cost-benefit appraisal of a specific investment project and the social valuation of its costs and benefits are implicitly being undertaken in the context of a partial equilibrium framework. In evaluating the economic impact of public sector investments, whether funded from the EU or from national exchequers, the appropriate analysis should take account of the general equilibrium effect of the investment. In practice this is very difficult to achieve, but it is essential to make some assumptions about the impact of an investment elsewhere on the economy. Here, as in so many other areas of investment appraisal, the judgment of the analyst will be important.

The partial versus general equilibrium analysis issue has an impact on a wide range of areas. One example is the impact of an investment decision on the economic return of other projects and the dangers of ignoring issues elsewhere in the economy that will have an impact on the net benefits of an investment. For example, the perceived net economic benefits of a specific road investment project (perhaps measured primarily in time savings) may be delayed or turn out to be illusory if there are bottlenecks elsewhere in the road network. Another example is where competing investments that are evaluated separately may overestimate the net benefits compared with an evaluation where each project is considered simultaneously. The converse situation also applies where the net benefits of two complementary projects may be greater when examined together.

For investments financed by structural funds, consideration of individual investment appraisals within a programme framework may assist in overcoming the problems associated with a partial equilibrium approach. This, however, requires in practice an understanding by the project analyst of the wider systems context for an investment. This is something that is not facilitated by fragmented departmental responsibilities within governments.

Comparison of Traded and Non-Traded Projects

One issue in economic cost-benefit appraisals that merits further consideration by economists is the comparison of investment opportunities between projects that are traded in the market and projects that are not traded. The introduction of market prices will usually serve to reduce demand. In such cases if shadow prices are used to measure the economic value of the benefits the estimated benefits may be lower than for similar projects where no market prices are applied and where the resultant demand is higher. This could, for example, apply to a comparison between non-toll and toll road projects. It is important that account be taken of the danger of any implicit bias in the application of economic cost-benefit methods in such cases. The potential problem here relates not to the basic approach of cost-benefit appraisals but to the possible overestimation of benefits using shadow prices. For example, the author suspects that standard methods of valuing benefits for transport investments in terms of time savings using wage rates may overestimate benefits. (See example 3.2 for a discussion of elements used to measure economic benefits of transport investments.) Another possible reason why such appraisals may in some cases overestimate the benefits is the failure to take account of the wider impact of the investment (see, for example, Hoehm and Randall, 1989).

*Example 3.2   Elements Used to Measure Economic Benefits of Transport
                Investments*

Many transport investment proposals are for projects where there are no
financial revenues (for example non-toll roads). Evaluating the merits of
such investments requires alternative measures of benefits. Even for those
transport investment projects where market revenues exist it may be
necessary to adjust market prices to derive an appropriate valuation of the
economic costs and benefits involved. It is useful to consider a number of
the elements that are frequently used to measure the economic benefits of
transport infrastructural projects. Where possible, revealed preferences
based on information from market prices should be used to measure the
value to consumers based on their willingness to pay. It is, however, often
difficult to derive reliable estimates for many of the non-market benefits
or costs of transport investments.

VALUATION OF REDUCED OR INCREASED CONGESTION

The valuation of reduced or increased congestion is often a key element
in the economic evaluation of transport infrastructural projects. For
example, reduced road congestion is often seen as one of the most
important economic benefits of new road investments or improvement
projects. The valuation of congestion is also used in the economic
assessment of railway investments, where reduced road congestion may
be one of the benefits. The disbenefits in the form of road congestion are
also used to evaluate the economic costs or benefits of retaining existing
rail or other transport services. This highlights the link between different
modes of transport and also the interdependence of different parts of the
transport network. Calculating the valuation of congestion may require
estimating a number of variables, including changes in vehicle speeds and
changes in vehicle operating costs. The calculation of the value of
reduced congestion would also require the preparation of traffic forecasts
and the estimation of vehicle occupancy figures and accident savings
costs.

A number of these factors are also used in combination with estimates of
the value of time to derive a valuation for congestion. Typically, in the case
of a road investment, in addition to estimating the specific features of the
investment in terms of speeds and traffic projections it would be necessary

to estimate time savings, reduction in accidents, vehicle cost savings, resource costs, environmental impacts, and wider costs or benefits.

Time savings: Time savings often represent the most important economic benefit of a transport investment. The value of time savings will depend on the alternative use of the traveller's time. By convention this is usually taken as equal to the wage rate before taxes for working time and at a lower level for leisure time. Different approaches are also used to measure waiting time compared with in-vehicle time. In the author's opinion there is a danger that some of the standard estimates used for measuring the value of time savings may overestimate the value to consumers based on their willingness to pay, and further research in the EU in this area would be justified.

Reduction in accident costs: A range of approaches has been used to derive estimates of the value of a reduction in the number of accidents and deaths, including insurance valuations and values based on estimates of willingness to take risks.

Vehicle cost savings: A reduction in travel time makes it possible for vehicle cost savings to be achieved, sometimes based on a fuel cost saving and a full operating cost saving, depending on the nature of the traffic. Standardised estimates are usually available.

Resource costs: Resource costs savings—for example savings in road maintenance or resource costs of substitute journeys or avoidable costs of providing a rail service—should be included in transport project appraisals.

Environmental impacts: While environmental impacts are increasingly being given attention in the evaluation of transport investments, these are very difficult to estimate, and in many small projects the environmental impact may be negligible. Environmental impact statements should cover the impact on the landscape, water, and air, noise, and solid waste.

Wider costs or benefits: For significant transport investments it is important to consider wider costs and benefits in terms of the impact on economic development. In practice it may not be possible to assign precise values to such wider impacts, but this may often not be a relevant issue in evaluating the merits of alternative projects.

3.2 THEORETICAL FOUNDATIONS

Cost-benefit appraisal of public sector investments is an approach to the evaluation in money terms of the costs and benefits of an investment from the community and social or economic perspective. The misuse and misinterpretation of cost-benefit analysis is usually a result of inappropriate assumptions on imputed prices or other aspects of the method or from a lack of knowledge of the use and limitations of this approach. It is therefore important to set the review of the cost-benefit method of investment appraisal against the background of a brief review of its theoretical foundations.

Theory of Welfare Economics

Cost-benefit appraisals of investment are based on the theory of welfare economics and are designed to promote rational choices between alternative projects from the viewpoint of the wider community, taking account of all the costs and benefits involved. The underlying assumption is that, in considering public sector investments, the overall objective is to ensure that the welfare of society is maximised, subject to constraints. In practice the welfare of society is usually considered in national terms, something that perhaps should be questioned in the context of investments financed by EU structural funds.

In fact much of welfare economics has been concerned with exploring the circumstances under which cost-benefit analysis would be unnecessary, namely when market prices would provide the correct signals for maximising economic well-being. According to fundamental theorems of welfare economics, this can only be expected when markets are perfectly competitive and achieve full-employment equilibrium. Even then only a limited form of optimality, known as Pareto optimality (from the Italian economist), is guaranteed. The Pareto criterion more or less ignores the question of income distribution, as an economy is at a Pareto optimum if there is no improvement that can be made without hurting someone. Still, if a Pareto improvement is possible (i.e. if the economy is not at a Pareto optimum), then it should be made.

Cost-benefit criteria are based on the concept of a potential Pareto improvement, i.e. a move that, though it might hurt some, would benefit others so much that they could compensate the losers. This concept, attributed to Kaldor and Hicks, is implemented in cost-benefit analysis by calculating the net discounted benefits. If these are positive, then the winners could pay the losers and still be better off.

There are two important caveats to be mentioned. First, since there is no assurance that the hypothetical compensating payments will be made, the use of the Kaldor-Hicks criterion could result in projects going ahead with undesirable distributional consequences. Second, account might need to be taken of the fact that the value of an extra pound at the margin may differ between different people, especially depending on their income or wealth.

While these caveats need to be taken very seriously in cost-benefit analysis for developing countries, it is perhaps reasonable to neglect them in the EU context, where governments already have relatively efficient mechanisms for redistributing income, especially through the tax system.

Consumer and Producer Surpluses

In a perfectly competitive economy, market prices of goods and services and factors of production would equal the marginal social value of their use. If an investment is not marginal, or if there are externalities, then the relevant social costs and benefits will be the resultant change arising from the investment in the consumers' and producers' surpluses. The valuation of the change in these surpluses at market prices will provide the appropriate estimation of the net benefits of the investment. In this context, consumer surplus is simply the amount that users or consumers would be willing to pay for goods or services arising from an investment, less the price they are charged. A producer surplus is the difference in profits for the producers between the initial and final situations under review.

Take the example of an investment project that will lower the price of a product from P_1 to P_2, assuming a linear demand curve (D), where Q_1 is the quantity demand at price P_1 (before the investment). Following the investment, the price falls to P_2 and the demand increases to Q_2.

The consumer surplus, which measures the excess of willingness to pay over price, increases by the shaded area. In this simple example, where there is a linear demand, the change in the consumer surplus is indicated by the formula Δ consumer surplus $= \Delta[\frac{1}{2}Q(P_0 - P)] = \frac{1}{2}(\Delta Q)(\Delta P) + Q\Delta P$. The level of generated demand (GD) is $\Delta Q = Q_2 - Q_1$. With a linear demand

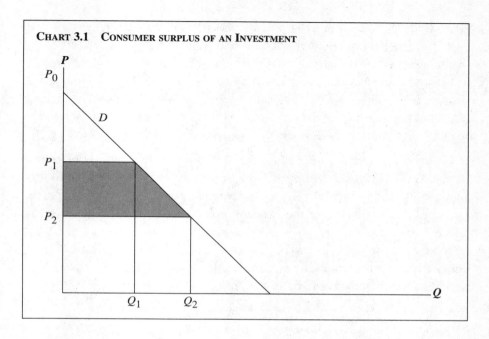

CHART 3.1 CONSUMER SURPLUS OF AN INVESTMENT

curve, the value of generated demand is equal to half the price change multiplied by the quantity change. This formula is important in estimating benefits in special circumstances where a linear demand curve is assumed to apply. This frequently applies in transport investments, where the gain in consumer surplus on the part of generated demand is assumed to be the difference between the maximum price this group would pay and the actual amount paid.

Distortions and Externalities

Whether an investment meets the economic efficiency criteria that underlie cost-benefit appraisal can be measured by comparing the relationship between the value of outputs or benefits and the value of inputs or costs. The value of output or benefits is, in simple terms, based on what consumers would be willing to pay, while the value of inputs is the price paid for the inputs by producers. This, however, needs to be modified to take account of externalities and of any distortions that mean that input prices do not reflect real economic resource costs.

Distortion refers to factors that cause a divergence between marginal social costs (or benefits) and market prices. Externalities refers to the effects of the investment on costs and benefits that do not directly accrue or are not directly allocated in the market pricing mechanism to the investment. Put simply, externalities are external effects that can also be termed secondary effects or spill-over effects. One of the externalities most frequently referred to is the impact of an investment on the environment.

It is therefore necessary to adjust market prices to take account of the external effects of the investment, but only where market prices fail to take account of these external effects. Externalities can arise from either the output of the investment or the expenditure associated with the investment. Externalities are in many cases non-marketable, because they often cannot be aimed at users and may involve a joint supply to multiple users. A cost-benefit analysis that took account of external costs and benefits attributable to parties not directly involved in the project is given in example 3.3.

Example 3.3   Cost-Benefit Analysis of a Tourism Investment in Italy:
the Example of the Pescara Marina

Pescara is an Italian city in the Abrizzo region on the Adriatic coast. In 1984 a project to create a marina in Pescara was proposed to the Ministry of Finance. After approval, 18 million ECU was invested in the construction of the marina. A preliminary evaluation was undertaken in 1984. The analysis considered the impact over a fifty-year period. A financial analysis forecast that the utilisation of moorings in the proposed marina would be 47 per cent starting from year 4, 65 per cent from year 5, and subsequently 90 per cent. An annual tariff of 640,000 lire per metre of marina was forecast, indicating a turnover after year 5 of 3.6 million ECU.

An economic-type analysis was also completed. This involved the exclusion of taxes and the application of a shadow price for labour equal to 67 per cent of the market cost of construction-related labour. The analysis also took account of what was referred to as external costs and benefits attributable to parties not directly involved in the project. These were assumed to include profits due to an increase in the tourism sector and profits due to an increase in turnover in the fishing sector through the use by fishing boats of the space in the old port previously used by pleasure boats. The analysis indicated a financial discounted NPV for the project of 38 million ECU and an economic discounted NPV of 109 million ECU. An estimated IRR of 5 per cent was calculated for the financial analysis and an IRR of 14 per cent for the economic or social cost-benefit analysis. A subsequent analysis of the project indicated that if the figures were adjusted to allow for a number of possible scenarios, the numbers decreased considerably, raising a question whether the net economic benefits were attractive enough.

Source: MEANS, Università Commerciale Luigi Bocconi (1994).

It is also necessary to adjust prices where market imperfections or monopoly practices exist in either goods or input markets. In these circumstances market prices diverge from true economic costs, and as a result valuations based on market pricing would result in divergence from Pareto-optimum situations. If these prices were not adjusted, inappropriate investment decisions would be likely to result. The existence of other factors, such as taxes and subsidies or increasing scale returns, may also imply that market prices do not reflect all the social costs and benefits. Shadow prices in such circumstances may therefore be needed because of the divergence between the marginal social costs (MSC) and marginal social values (MSV) of the relevant commodities. Unless the price or value of the benefits of an investment equal their marginal costs, the optimum allocation of resources will not be achieved.

Shadow prices may also need to be used when there are inherent reasons for market failure, as in the case of social goods.

The existence of unemployed resources is one of the main reasons for the use of shadow prices or opportunity costs. In the presence of conditions of less than full employment there is likely to be a discrepancy between market prices and social or opportunity costs. An excess supply in relation to demand for any resource suggests that market prices may overstate the economic cost of using that resource. The issue is, however, far from simple, and the use of adjusted or shadow prices for unemployed resources is one of the most difficult and controversial aspects of economic cost-benefit appraisals. (This issue is considered in more detail in section 4.2, where the shadow price for labour is discussed.)

3.3 Basic Elements

The practical steps in investment appraisal are outlined in chapter 8. It is, however, useful to summarise here some of the basic elements of cost-benefit analysis. These include the following:

- Identification of all costs of the investment, including both direct and indirect costs. Costs are usually considered as the investment expenditure on a project but may also include negative impacts or disbenefits arising from an investment.

- Identification of all the benefits of the project. Benefits relate to the favourable impacts or outputs of the project.

- Assigning monetary values to all costs and benefits that reflect their social values.

The task of assigning monetary values to costs and benefits is the most difficult element of cost and benefit evaluations, usually involving an estimation of how the investment will affect society's welfare by inferring the values. This is done by analysing consumer behaviour or by other approaches and involves the use of opportunity costs or shadow pricing. An example of the application of this approach to the economic evaluation of a motorway investment is presented in example 3.4. (Because of the importance and the difficulties of this task, it is discussed in detail in chapter 4. Comparing the sum of the discounted costs and benefits is discussed in chapter 5.)

---

*Example 3.4   Economic Evaluation of a Motorway Investment:
            the Example of the Naas Bypass*

Naas is the junction point of two national primary road routes. The motorway bypass cost 19.8 million ECU at 1983 prices and involved the construction of the motorway as well as road bridges and approach roads, interchanges, and an underpass. An economic analysis of the investment was published in 1984 and followed the traditional U.K. practice in the

---

evaluation of time savings, differentiating between leisure and working time. Fatal accident costs were based on U.K. published estimates. Estimated average speed of traffic produced forty-one estimates of journey time, and a weighted average of the journey times was estimated. This was applied to traffic projections to derive aggregate time savings estimates, which were based on assumptions for occupancy factors. As well as time savings and accident cost savings, the third quantified benefit from the investment was savings in fuel consumption. These were based on the assumptions for speed used in the analysis of time savings.

The economic analysis evaluated the time stream of benefits and costs over twenty years. The analysis indicated an internal rate of return of 20.51 per cent, assuming a 2 per cent annual growth in traffic and national income. Time savings accounted for most of the estimated benefits (90.6 per cent). A sensitivity analysis was also undertaken, which showed that the project had a 6.84 per cent rate of return even with a pessimistic scenario of zero traffic and income growth and zero value of leisure time applied to 83 per cent of cars.

The environmental aspects of the investment were seen as positive in the form of a reduction in noise, smoke, and lead pollution. Some negative environmental costs were identified but were judged to be probably much less than the environmental costs caused by traffic in the absence of the investment.

Source: Barrett and Mooney (1984).

4

THE USE OF OPPORTUNITY COSTS OR SHADOW PRICING

Opportunity costs or economic costs represent the value of resources in their most valuable alternative uses. The opportunity costs are sometimes referred to as social costs and measure the opportunity cost of the resources in the best alternative use that is forgone. Shadow prices are simply the specific estimated prices used in cost-benefit evaluations where it is assumed that market prices do not reflect economic or opportunity costs, or where no prices exist. Originally shadow prices were used only to estimate the value of a benefit or cost where market distortions existed, but in general they now also refer to values of non-traded products.

4.1 RATIONALE FOR USE

Financial advisers and policy-makers frequently ask why it is necessary in the evaluation of EU-funded or other public sector investments to use opportunity or shadow pricing rather than market costs or prices in economic investment appraisals. However, as mentioned previously, market prices rather than estimated shadow prices should be used unless they are not available or there are clear reasons why they are not appropriate. It is also frequently desirable to undertake a financial appraisal and an economic appraisal of an investment simultaneously. In these cases a comparison of the financial appraisal (which provides a market judgment on a project) and the economic appraisal that employs opportunity costs or shadow prices provides an implicit indication of the estimated degree of market distortions and externalities. This is often not possible, however, as many investments produce benefits that are not priced directly in the market. In other cases, even where the output of an investment is traded, market imperfections and externalities prevent market prices being the appropriate measure of the opportunity costs of resources or the appropriate value of the benefits of the investments. Example 4.1 shows the application of shadow prices to a British railway investment.

Example 4.1 Evaluation of Social Benefits and Finances of a Rail Investment: the Victoria Line Example

The Victoria Line is an urban railway line linking Victoria Station with north-east London. An urban rail improvement involving the construction of an underground railway on the line was evaluated by two economists, Foster and Beesley, and the decision to authorise its construction was made by the government. The initial economic analysis suggested that the discounted NPV of the investment was positive. The analysis indicated three main benefits: time savings, savings in operating costs, and the value of comfort and convenience arising from the investment.

Time savings were estimated to be the most important economic benefit. Some revised figures presented by the economists showed that in present value terms there was a social or economic benefit of about 41 million ECU from the rail investment, although the project recorded an overall financial loss in NPV terms of about 28 million ECU. This loss was derived from an estimated NPV cost of construction of 49 million ECU, less a net gain on operating costs of 13 million ECU and a railway-wide net gain of 8 million ECU. The analysis assumed a fifty-year life span, 5½ years' construction, and a 6 per cent discount rate.

The subsequent analysis undertaken by the economists also suggested that the way in which the investment would be financed could affect the valuation of the social costs and benefits. For example, it was estimated that increasing average fares over the whole of the London rail network to replace the financial losses of the project would lead to reduced benefits to the extent of 40–61 per cent of the estimated gains. This would arise because of the probable loss of passengers as a result of the fare increase. It was estimated that because of the diversion of travellers from the underground there would be gains to those remaining that might decrease the losses by between one-fifteenth and one-twenty-fourth at the maximum.

Sources: Foster and Beesley (1963), Beesley and Foster (1965).

Start with Market Prices where Possible

Not all social or opportunity costs differ from market values, and in circumstances where they equate there is no need for shadow prices except for measuring the value of benefits where they are not traded in the market. In many instances opportunity costs may be the same as or very similar to market prices. In such cases market prices will provide an appropriate valuation of costs and benefits. In the absence of any evident significant market distortions, actual market prices are probably the best estimate of opportunity costs. The rationale for the use of shadow pricing, however, applies where unemployment or uncompetitive market practices exist, causing a divergence between market prices and social or opportunity costs. They are also used where no market prices exist. As discussed in chapter 3 (where the theoretical foundations for cost-benefit analysis were briefly discussed), the rationale for the use of shadow prices is the desire to ensure that investments meet the economic efficiency or national income criterion. The central task in deciding on the merits of investments is the efficiency of the allocation of resources in the economy. The function of shadow prices is, therefore, to provide resource valuations or substitution ratios between alternative uses so that the economy is able to achieve economic efficiency.

Reasons Why Market Prices May Not Be Appropriate

Market prices may not reflect the desired economic opportunity costs, for a number of reasons. These include market imperfections, such as restrictive practices; also relevant are government subsidies and taxes, unemployed resources, and externalities. In the case of distortions arising from restrictive practices, it is useful to consider whether the restrictions are likely to remain. Similar issues arise where monopolistic suppliers exist, resulting in prices above marginal costs or competitive price levels. If output is expected to be increased by the monopoly supplier as a result of the investment, an adjustment to market prices will be necessary. Where a national government is the supplier, market prices may simply reflect historical or administrative decisions and may be below or above economic opportunity costs (see example 4.2). This example also highlights the fact that a number of costs, such as depreciation or financial charges, should be excluded from any economic or financial evaluation of future options.

Example 4.2 National Resource Allocation and Shadow Prices: an Example of a European Fertiliser Plant

A state-owned fertiliser manufacturing plant in a small EU country was allocated natural gas by the government from a gas field that was discovered in 1973. The gas was used to manufacture ammonia, which was in turn used to manufacture a nitrogen fertiliser. At the start of the 1980s the company was experiencing financial difficulties and had not been able to record a net profit in any recent year, despite the views of some commentators that the price of gas sold to the company was below its economic value.

In 1983 an economic analysis was undertaken that, among other things, evaluated alternatives for the future of the company. The method employed was to use financial data based on actual prices and costs and to analyse the alternative uses of natural gas. Adjustments were then made to incorporate broader economic factors.

The analysis focused on adjusting the price of gas charged to the company to reflect its economic opportunity cost, i.e. the price that would represent the full resource cost of allocating it to one use rather than another. This essentially involved evaluating the economic contribution of alternative uses of the gas, based on market prices for the output and the costs of non-gas inputs required. The analysis used the concept of gas threshold values (GTVs), which was estimated for each potential use of the gas and was defined as the maximum value of an additional therm of gas to the user, which equals the total additional revenue or cost savings to the user from using one further unit of gas, less the additional non-gas costs incurred. This was estimated at an average threshold value per therm to identified outlets of 0.37–0.40 ECU; in the longer term it was estimated to fall in the range 0.31–0.40 ECU. The GTVs for use in the fertiliser plant varied by product. For ammonia products it was estimated to be in the range 0.18–0.30 ECU; for other products it was estimated to be in the range 0.25–0.47 ECU. The analysis suggested that from a national economic point of view ammonia output should be reduced, even though this would increase financial losses at the company. It also suggested that the future of the ammonia complex should be monitored and that if the threshold value of gas were to fall and remain below the best alternative use of the gas, the complex should be closed. The analysis also subtracted depreciation and financial charges from the analysis, as they were sunk costs.

An analysis of the economy-wide impact of alternative uses of gas in terms of environmental effects, direct and indirect employment effects, balance of payment effects, forward linkages and security of supply was also undertaken. The analysis concluded that for each impact the social costs and benefits were small relative to the company's financial results, and the difference between these effects and those that would flow from alternative uses of the gas was even smaller.

This case study highlights a number of important aspects of economic appraisals. Of interest is the validity of ignoring sunk capital costs in deciding on future options. This of course would not and should not apply at the time of the initial capital appraisal. Investment expenditures once incurred are often irretrievable, but this does not take away from the fact that initial investments that do not produce a return represent a misallocation of resources. A second point of interest is the fact that 'market' prices, if determined by historical or administrative decisions rather than on the basis of a competitive market, may underestimate economic opportunity costs.

Source: Blackwell, Convery, Walsh, and Walsh (1983).

Need for National Guidelines on Key Assumptions

A number of key decisions about shadow prices will be common to a variety of different project appraisals. These include questions related to the treatment of taxation, the social discount rate, and the shadow prices of labour. These are all difficult questions, on which there is no uniformity of opinion.

To the extent that different projects are competing for funds from a common pool (as is the case with the structural funds), consistency of treatment is desirable, even if the promoters of the project are different, as will often be the case where projects are in different parts of the country. In such circumstances, therefore, guidelines should be provided at the decision-making level on the approach to be adopted. These guidelines need not always be provided by central government but should be drawn up at an appropriate level of decision-making.

The treatment of taxation is a good example here. When indirect taxes are imposed by central government for the purpose of raising revenue, they drive a wedge between price and marginal cost. Decisions taken on the basis of tax-inclusive prices, therefore, may not be in accordance with marginal cost. Nevertheless, private enterprises and households are making such decisions every day. For the cost-benefit analyst to make project evaluations on the basis of tax-exclusive prices is to treat these projects differently from private projects. The wedge thereby introduced between private and public projects may be as distorting as that between price and marginal cost.

Furthermore, many indirect taxes have a corrective effect: they adjust the market price for some other distortion. It would be wrong to exclude corrective taxes from the shadow prices used in cost-benefit analysis.

Since it is the central government that sets rates of tax, the best practical approach would seem to be for the government to determine for what types of project and for what types of taxation shadow prices should be included on a tax-exclusive basis. If the central government makes no such adjudication, the lower level of government that is assessing the cost-benefit has no basis for deviating from tax-inclusive prices.

A practical rule of thumb for taxation would be for central governments to recommend ignoring indirect taxes (i.e. those on production or trade) but to take account of direct taxes (on income or capital)—in other words, to measure taxed inputs at factor costs. Similarly, direct subsidies should be excluded. This is, however, largely a question of measurement convenience and is not altogether satisfactory. Another area where national guidelines are required is in relation to the shadow price of labour. Some of the issues that would face policy-makers in determining guidelines in this area are discussed in the following section.

4.2 OPPORTUNITY COST OF LABOUR

Rationale for Adjusting Market Labour Costs

One of the most important technical issues in shadow pricing for economic investment appraisals in EU countries concerns whether to adjust the market price for labour and, if so, by how much. Given the levels of unemployment in EU countries, the levels of total labour costs, including taxes, are unlikely to equal the social opportunity costs of labour in member-states. The social opportunity cost of labour in investment appraisal refers to the value of the alternative employment that the individuals employed as a result of the investment could find without displacing other people in the labour market.

If there is involuntary unemployment and if one assumes that there are no indirect or macro-economic implications of employing individuals associated with the investment (e.g. impact on labour costs, inflation, etc.), the appropriate economic cost is not the labour cost but rather the value of the leisure forgone. This element could be negative if the value of employment, per se, is high.

It has, however, been argued that as a result of other policy decisions, governments have decided on the level of unemployment, and, as a result, no adjustments should be made to the market prices for labour costs. It is also sometimes suggested that any perceived macro-economic benefit arising from exchequer savings on unemployment benefit could be obtained from the use of the expenditure on the investment in other ways. In practice, however, in most EU countries for certain periods there is structural unemployment, and some adjustments to labour costs may be required.

Difficulties in Deciding on Appropriate Values

The difficulties in deciding on the treatment of labour costs in investment appraisals in circumstances of unemployment include whether (if adjustments are being made) to adjust direct or indirect labour inputs. For example, should only the price of labour directly associated with a project be adjusted or should the labour cost element in other aspects of the costs of materials, equipment and services be adjusted as well? If adjustments are only made for direct employment associated with the project, what are the implications for the efficient allocation of resources? For example, if only direct labour costs are adjusted, would this inappropriately bias investments against projects with significant indirect employment spin-offs?

As indicated previously in the general discussion of the rationale for the use of shadow prices, an important aspect is whether the resources will be unemployed at the time of their use in the proposed investment. This is often difficult to forecast, particularly over a long time, and in certain countries can be significantly determined by the growth prospects in adjoining member-states where migration can result in close interactions between labour markets. With the increasing integration of EU countries and the removal of barriers to labour mobility between member-states, this factor is likely to grow in importance. In circumstances where the employment aspects of a project are long-term as well as short-term and it is expected that employment prospects are likely to improve, this factor needs to be taken into account. This may mean assigning higher opportunity costs to longer-term employment associated with the investment.

Use of Empirical Evidence and Alternative Policy Options

Deciding on the actual values for use in the shadow pricing of unemployed resources can, in practice, be guided by examining empirical evidence or by evaluating prices implied by other public sector policies. The latter approach takes account of the fact that governments in member-states have a range of policy options other than specific investment decisions for responding to unemployment.

Another issue that is relevant in deciding on the opportunity cost of labour is the impact of the funding of an investment on taxation. This applies equally to projects based on EU structural funds and borrowings with no direct taxation. This is because it is sensible to assume that alternative uses for the funds could be found. This applies even where the additionality criterion is relevant.

Importance of Opportunity Cost of Labour

The issue of the opportunity cost of labour is of key practical importance in investment appraisals. In the author's experience, when the output or benefits of an investment are marketable, differences between the market price of labour and its estimated economic opportunity cost frequently represent the largest element of the economic benefit of investment projects. Despite the validity of some of the arguments referred to above (alternative uses of funds, implied policy decisions, treatment of indirect labour inputs, etc.), which suggest the need for caution against including a zero or low value for labour costs in investment appraisal, it would not be sensible to use market rates for the labour input if the output (or construction) of the investment was attributable to individuals who would otherwise be unemployed. The task of deciding on national guidelines for appropriate shadow prices for labour should, therefore, be guided by an assessment of this key issue.

Observed prices for labour costs are undoubtedly a misleading guide to true opportunity costs when, at these prices, part of the labour market is involuntarily unemployed. In such cases the economic opportunity cost of using labour inputs will not be correctly reflected in the market costs of these resources.

In principle, even if there is no alternative use for the labour input, adjustment should be made for the value of employment versus the value of leisure forgone. In practice, it may be very difficult if not impossible to provide sensible estimates on this factor.

Treatment of Overtime and Impact of Project on Overall Labour Costs

In calculating actual shadow prices for labour, the extent to which overtime payments are included should be considered where possible. In general, it is suggested that overtime payments should be included as having a 100 per cent, or near-100 per cent, opportunity cost. Also relevant is the impact of an investment on overall labour costs in the market and the consequences of this for employment elsewhere in the economy. If a new investment bids up labour costs, then, even if the project employs resources that would otherwise have been unemployed, there may be reductions in employment in other activities arising from the cost increase. This is particularly important where skilled labour may be involved. To the extent that the new investment is in a high-technology, capital-intensive area, the danger of a negative employment impact will be greater if the investment results in increases in labour costs in more labour-intensive parts of the economy. This indicates that even in the special circumstances where the labour cost was attributable to individuals who would otherwise be unemployed, assigning a zero shadow price to labour may not be appropriate.

Labour Market Conditions and Skill Levels

The task of developing guidelines for appropriate shadow prices for labour might also usefully take account of the location of the investment and whether a national or regional analysis is being undertaken. In general, cost-benefit analysis should be considered at a national level, although regional labour market factors may have an impact on the shadow prices used in a specific investment appraisal. Shadow prices for labour should also ideally take account of skill levels. For example, an investment project in a regional area with very high levels of unemployment might assign a shadow price for unskilled labour at or near zero, while skilled labour that would be attracted from other regions may have a value at, or near, market levels. Semi-skilled employment may have an opportunity cost somewhere in between these levels. In practice, it is often assumed that the market price for skilled labour reflects the opportunity costs or marginal productivity; however, this is not always the case. In some countries, where unemployment is high and there is an educated unemployed labour force, skill shortages may not be so common and may be primarily short-term in nature. In such cases differentiation on a skill basis may be less appropriate.

The wider impact of assuming a zero or very low opportunity cost for labour in the context of public sector investments needs careful consideration. One reason why this is relevant is that if all public sector investments were implemented where the cost-benefit ratio was positive after assigning a zero shadow price for labour, there would undoubtedly be an unsustainably high investment programme, which could well be far greater than required to meet full employment targets.

As suggested above, the task of choosing an appropriate shadow price for labour should be guided by a judgment on whether the output of the investments was attributable to individuals who would otherwise be unemployed. This will be influenced by unemployment rates. However, the existence of involuntary unemployment in itself does not indicate that these circumstances will prevail. If the employees associated with the construction or subsequent output of an investment project were previously employed elsewhere in the economy, there would be no increase in employment, unless the employees' previous positions were replaced or unless their previous employment was due to be terminated in the absence of the investment. A zero opportunity cost would assume not only very high levels of existing and future unemployment but also that there will be no negative labour market or macro-economic impacts arising from the investment. A zero opportunity cost for labour implies that, as a result of the investment, and taking account of both direct and indirect impacts, there will be a 100 per cent sustainable addition to output and employment. This implies that all the extra employees will be drawn from the unemployed, or will come from other employment that will be fully replaced by unemployed workers, and that there will be no loss of output elsewhere in the economy. It assumes no opportunity costs on the value of leisure forgone. The issue of the characteristics of the labour input to investment projects is important, as there are marked differences in the level and duration of unemployment by skill categories, by age, and by regional location. Also relevant is the degree of labour force mobility between regions; and in the context of investments financed by EU structural funds, the degree of labour mobility between member-states may be of interest. This factor is likely to vary by country and by skill category.

Lack of a One-to-One Relationship between Employment and Unemployment

In formulating national guidelines for the opportunity cost of labour, account must be taken of evidence in the EU countries that suggests that an expansion of employment will not result in a corresponding equal reduction in the level of unemployment. To assess the significance of this for the shadow pricing of labour it is necessary to consider the reason why a greater number of additional jobs is required to reduce the level of unemployment by a given amount. If this is because the employment created as a result of a new investment affects labour costs and causes redundancies or repressed vacancies, then clearly assuming a zero opportunity cost for labour would be inappropriate.

It is difficult to imagine that significant public sector investments, or publicly assisted private sector investments, have not had some effect on local wage levels and thereby indirectly on employment elsewhere in the economy. If, however, the investment encourages immigration or a return of emigrants from another EU country, then the issue is somewhat more complex and would depend on whether the cost-benefit appraisal is being undertaken from the perspective of the member-state or from the viewpoint of the impact on the EU economy. It will also depend on whether those employed in the project were previously unemployed in other countries. In practice, cost-benefit appraisals of investments involving EU structural funds are evaluated in national terms, in the same way as other public sector investments. As a result the labour costs associated with inward migration should be priced at market levels. In certain circumstances, inward migration may provide additional benefits to the economy in the form of skills or an entrepreneurial culture. These benefits may be significant in the long term but are very difficult to assess as part of a formal investment appraisal.

Another reason why additional employment may not have an equal impact on unemployment levels is that it may encourage labour force participation rates to increase. This would suggest that the investment may have had a greater impact on real unemployment levels than is indicated by official unemployment statistics. In such cases, while the exchequer impact will be different, the economic impact will be the same as if official unemployment declined, except to the extent to which the economic value of leisure forgone may be different between the unemployed and new entrants to the labour force who were encouraged as a result of the investment.

Choosing the Appropriate Shadow Price

In practice, determining appropriate shadow prices for labour may require details on the labour input to the construction stage and subsequent output for certain types of proposed investments. It may also require very detailed information on the existing and forecast features of national or local labour markets. Some of this information is collected by national labour force surveys and Eurostat. Supplementary information is usually available as a result of ad hoc surveys or specific analyses undertaken for other purposes.

The extent to which detailed empirical research on specific labour market issues is justified would depend, in part, on the size of the proposed investment and the significance of changes in the relevant variables on the overall project. The choice should, however, be determined within a range set by national guidelines, and in most cases specific project-related research will not be justified. Indeed, as indicated previously, there are dangers of a lack of consistency in individual analysts attempting to derive estimates for the shadow price of labour.

Factors Influencing the Choice of the Shadow Price of Labour

The analysis in this chapter suggests that there can be no fixed estimate of the shadow price for labour and that the appropriate value will be influenced by the following factors, a number of which are interrelated:

- The national level of unemployment
- The forecasts for future levels of unemployment and labour force growth rates
- The skill levels and other labour force characteristics
- The degree to which skill shortages exist
- The regional location of the project and the local labour market features
- The degree of national and international labour force mobility
- The extent to which the project causes a loss of output or employment elsewhere in the economy
- The extent of direct versus indirect labour inputs
- The degree to which labour costs represent wage levels or taxes
- The extent of overtime assumed
- The level of taxes and subsidies involved

The level of opportunity cost for labour could vary between 0 and 100 per cent. Indeed shadow price levels above 100 per cent of market prices could apply if market prices reflect training or other implicit subsidies. In practice, the national unemployment rate is probably the minimum percentage of labour inputs that would have no opportunity cost, and it is hard or impossible to conceive of circumstances where 100 per cent or nearly 100 per cent of the labour force associated with a project in the EU would have no opportunity cost. Deciding on where in between these levels to set the shadow price for labour would require detailed research and should be determined by national guidelines. In most cases an opportunity cost for labour of between 40 and 90 per cent of market prices may be appropriate.

5

DISCOUNTING COSTS AND BENEFITS

5.1 Definition of Discounting

Benefits or costs that arise at different periods cannot be directly compared without taking account of the time value of money, as represented by the rate of interest or discount.

A central task in both financial and economic project appraisals is to estimate the 'present value' of the costs and benefits of an investment. This is undertaken by discounting the costs and benefits back to the specified period. The period is usually the present but could be the year in which the project will start or some other specified period.

Discounting is the basis for adjusting future monetary values to a standard equivalent value. In other words, it represents the technique of converting future monetary values to their equivalent value in today's terms. Its purpose is to make it feasible to aggregate all costs and benefits that arise at different times.

Discounting involves using a specified interest or discount rate that enables one to translate the estimated future net benefits of an investment in value terms to the valuation in terms of an earlier period. Discounting is therefore a way of capitalising the value of a stream of future net benefits. (An overview of the techniques for undertaking this task was presented in chapter 2.)

Discounting is needed because investments usually involve costs and benefits that occur at different times. Typically an investment project will involve initial capital costs, with benefits and operating costs and possibly additional capital costs occurring at later periods. The task of comparing costs and benefits that arise in different periods can only be undertaken by discounting the value of these costs and benefits at different values, depending on when they occur.

Discounting is implemented by the use of a discount rate. The discount or interest rate is simply the numerical value that relates costs or benefits in one period to those in another. The discount rate used should represent a 'real' interest rate (after adjusting for inflation) and should be applied to costs and benefits expressed in real terms, i.e. not nominal flows.

5.2 PURPOSE OF DISCOUNTING

In considering EU or other public sector expenditure proposals, probably the best way to explain the purpose or rationale of discounting is to say that it takes account of the cost of servicing national debt. In practice the real alternative use of exchequer revenues in member-states (whether transfers from the EU or revenues raised through taxes or other means) is to repay government debt. In practical terms this provides the clearest reason why it is necessary to discount investment projects.

Alternative Rationales

In economic investment appraisals, discounting is often explained by other complex reasons, including the need to take account of the social marginal time preference rate. But in practice these come down to the same thing, as they will in turn be related to the market rate of interest being paid on the government debt.

The use or purpose of the discount rate in public sector project appraisals is sometimes justified by the need to adjust future costs or benefits for the weighting or preference for benefits now rather than later. This is referred to as the social time preference rate. Some economists have suggested that part of the individual time preference rate may be irrational and that this factor should be adjusted by governments. This is based on a belief that the future is more uncertain and less valued by individuals than it is by society. This may result, in part, from the obvious fact of limited life expectancy for individuals. It is generally accepted that the social time preference rate may fall short of the individual or private rate. The other purpose of discounting is an attempt to take account of the opportunity cost of capital, sometimes referred to as the social cost of capital. This is related to the rationale of the cost of servicing national debt and involves the use of a discount rate to take account of the best alternative use of the capital resources.

In circumstances of a perfect capital market, the social time preference rate and the opportunity cost of capital may be equated. In addition to the two purposes of discounting referred to above—to take account of society's time preference and the social opportunity cost of capital—discounting is also sometimes used to take account of risk. There are, however, theoretical and other issues involved in including a premium for risk in the discount rate. (A discussion of the handling of risks is presented in chapter 6.)

Significance of Discounting

The significance of discounting increases the longer the period over which the cost and benefits are compared. Discounting therefore involves scaling down the value of benefits that occur in the future.

Discounting has important practical uses in deciding between projects, for example in deciding between investments with high capital costs or low operating costs and projects with lower estimated capital requirements but with relative operating cost penalties, or projects where there are differences in the timing of benefits. The impact of discounting can be seen from the simple comparisons presented in example 5.1. Discounting is also important in deciding on the merits of individual projects by comparing the discounted NPVs.

Example 5.1 The Impact of Discounting

This is a comparison of two capital investment projects, each requiring capital costs of 2 million ECU and each discounted at two alternative discount rates, of 3 and 10 per cent. Project A has an undiscounted cumulative cash flow of 2 million ECU, while project B has an undiscounted cumulative cash flow of 2.25 million ECU. On an undiscounted basis, project B would appear superior; however, most of the undiscounted net benefits for this project occur after eleven years, while for project A the annual undiscounted net benefits are constant. When discounted rates are applied, the findings indicate that even at a low discount rate of 3 per cent, project A is more desirable. The example also shows that if a very high discount rate of 10 per cent is used, neither project produces a net economic benefit, but in this case the degree to which project B is less attractive is even more pronounced.

PROJECT A

Year	Cash flow	Present value discount factor (0.03)	Present value equivalent	Present value discount factor (0.10)	Present value equivalent
0	-2,000,000	1.0	-2,000,000	1.0	-2,000,000
1	+200,000	0.9709	194,180	0.9091	181,820
2	+200,000	0.9426	188,520	0.8264	165,280
3	+200,000	0.9151	183,020	0.7513	150,260
4	+200,000	0.8885	177,700	0.6830	136,600
5	+200,000	0.8626	172,520	0.6209	124,180
6	+200,000	0.8375	167,500	0.5645	112,900
7	+200,000	0.8131	162,620	0.5132	102,640
8	+200,000	0.7894	157,880	0.4665	93,300
9	+200,000	0.7664	153,280	0.4241	84,820
10	+200,000	0.7441	148,820	0.3855	77,100
11	+200,000	0.7224	144,480	0.3505	70,100
12	+200,000	0.7014	140,280	0.3186	63,720
13	+200,000	0.6810	136,200	0.2897	57,940
14	+200,000	0.6611	132,220	0.2633	52,660
15	+200,000	0.6419	128,380	0.2394	47,880
16	+200,000	0.6232	124,640	0.2176	43,520
17	+200,000	0.6050	121,000	0.1978	39,560
18	+200,000	0.5874	117,480	0.1799	35,980
19	+200,000	0.5703	114,060	0.1635	32,700
20	+200,000	0.5537	110,740	0.1486	29,720
NPV		at 3%	975,520	at 10%	-297,320

PROJECT B

Year	Cash flow	Present value discount factor (0.03)	Present value equivalent	Present value discount factor (0.10)	Present value equivalent
0	-2,000,000	1.0	-2,000,000	1.0	-2,000,000
1	+100,000	0.9709	97,090	0.9091	90,910
2	+100,000	0.9426	94,260	0.8264	82,640
3	+100,000	0.9151	91,510	0.7513	75,130
4	+100,000	0.8885	88,850	0.6830	68,300
5	+100,000	0.8626	86,200	0.6209	62,090
6	+100,000	0.8375	83,750	0.5645	56,450
7	+100,000	0.8131	81,310	0.5132	51,320
8	+100,000	0.7894	78,840	0.4665	46,650
9	+100,000	0.7664	76,640	0.4241	42,410
10	+100,000	0.7441	74,410	0.3855	38,550
11	+100,000	0.7224	32,240	0.3505	35,050
12	+350,000	0.7014	245,490	0.3186	111,510
13	+350,000	0.6810	238,350	0.2897	101,395
14	+350,000	0.6611	231,385	0.2633	92,155
15	+350,000	0.6419	224,665	0.2394	83,790
16	+350,000	0.6232	218,120	0.2176	76,160
17	+350,000	0.6050	211,750	0.1978	69,230
18	+350,000	0.5874	205,590	0.1799	62,965
19	+350,000	0.5703	199,605	0.1635	57,225
20	+350,000	0.5537	193,795	0.1486	52,010
NPV		at 3%	893,950	at 10%	-644,060

5.3 CHOICE OF DISCOUNT RATES

An important practical issue in evaluating public sector investment proposals is the choice of the discount rate. It has been suggested that no single discount rate can be found that will measure both the social time preference rate and the opportunity cost of capital. This has some merit if discounting is attempting to take account of a number of different factors, as discussed above. It has led some economists to suggest that a shadow price should be applied to capital resources and that the discount rate should be used only to reflect the social time preference function. In practice, however, there is a need for a single discount rate to be used to ensure consistency in investment decisions and ease of estimation. The issue arises therefore of how this rate should be chosen. There are essentially two approaches that can be followed: to base it on the market rate of interest, or to use some measure of society's time preference rate.

Market Rate of Interest

The market rate of interest has a practical merit in that it is possible to identify an observed rate that could be used, for example the long-term real rate of return on equity investments. This could be thought to represent the marginal efficiency of private sector investment opportunities or the private sector opportunity cost of capital. It therefore provides some measure of the opportunity costs of private sector investment that are forgone. It can also be argued that, since market rates balance the supply and demand for funds, they too implicitly take account of time preference issues.

Using market interest rates to discount public sector investments raises the question whether to adjust market rates to remove the impact of taxes. (A discussion of the treatment of taxation in opportunity costs was presented in chapter 4.) Adjustment for tax may be appropriate to the extent to which it increases required gross rates of return in the private sector.

In addition to these factors, the market rate on equity also takes account of the commercial risks involved. This factor could be largely removed by considering long-run returns on government gilts or bonds, although other factors are likely to be relevant in this measure, including the fact that these returns are sometimes set as part of monetary policy.

If a market rate of interest is accepted as appropriate, this still leaves open the issue of how it should be defined. Should it be the rate of return on equities and, if so, in what markets and over what periods? Should it be the cost at which governments can borrow funds? Or should it be the interest rate on private sector large time deposits, reflecting the willingness of depositors to forgo present consumption?

Use of Society's Time Preference Rate

If a market rate of interest is rejected, the main alternative concerns a measure of society's time preference rate. There are two problems with this. Firstly, there is the theoretical issue of how to adjust individual time preference rates to take account of the fact that these may overcompensate for society's preferences. Secondly, and more important in practice, is how to provide an actual measure of these preferences. One approach would be to attempt to identify an average long-term risk-adjusted rate. However, this brings one back to some definition of market rates. Possible alternative approaches could involve a government decision based on policy priorities, a rate based on observing a range of private sector trade-offs, and a rate based on stated preference market research. None of these approaches is fully satisfactory, and all have serious constraints in terms of actual measurement. If it is assumed that the social time preference rate relates to individuals' life expectancy evaluation, it may be possible to derive rates based on actuarial tables, but this is unlikely to be appropriate.

Two Practical Options

Despite the difficulties that exist in deciding on a discount rate, it is clear that some discount rate must be used. To abandon discounting would of course be simply to choose a zero discount rate implicitly. In practice a number of approaches have been followed in the choice of discount rates used in cost-benefit studies in EU countries. The two main approaches suggested are:

    (i) long-term rate on private sector equity investments

    (ii) rate of interest on government borrowing.

The use of the long-run real return on private sector equity investments (after adjustment for income taxes) provides some measure, albeit an imperfect one, of the opportunity cost of capital compared with private sector investment opportunities. This reflects the potential displacement of private sector investment opportunities by EU or other public sector funded investments. However, it is often felt that the return on equities is considerably higher (over the long run) than the yield on government bonds. It is hard to explain this differential in terms of the different risks involved.

Merits of Rate of Government Borrowings

The use of the rate of interest on government borrowing has the merit of providing some measure of the rate necessary to attract capital from other areas. This must, however, be adjusted for inflation and income taxes.

In the author's judgment the best approach is to use the rate of interest on government borrowings. In general, it may be desirable in practice to use a range of discount rates related to the interest rate on such borrowings. Current experience in EU countries would suggest that the use of real discount rates in the range 3–8 per cent may be appropriate.

6

HANDLING OF RISK

6.1 NATURE OF RISK

In evaluating public sector projects, one of the main issues that must be considered is how to handle risk. Risk in this general context refers to the danger that some of the assumptions underlying the project evaluation will not be realised. Many of the same issues arise in evaluating the commercial viability of projects.

Two of the greatest risks in investment appraisal are the risks associated with the forecasting of demand and with the estimation of capital costs. These represent what could be referred to as non-technical pitfalls in project evaluations. Because of their importance they are discussed separately in chapter 7.

Risk is sometimes defined more precisely as the chance of some outcome occurring, and it can be used to define the possibility or probability of some outcome. This technical definition refers to the likelihood of different outcomes occurring. It involves asking what is the probability of variance in the estimates of the input data.

Risk is also sometimes used to refer to the dangers associated with uncertainty. Uncertainty can be used to define a greater lack of information concerning the future. In this context it is sometimes equated with an unforeseeable or random circumstance and could be described as 'anyone's guess'. This would suggest that probabilities can be associated with risks but not with uncertainties. In practice it is necessary to distinguish between forecast bias and future uncertainty. It is essential that where possible, forecast bias is removed from project appraisals.

Recent research on World Bank projects before and after completion indicate that the initial appraisals were in general too optimistic (see example 6.1). Also of interest is the fact that conventional factors such as

68

cost overruns and implementation delays seem to explain only a small part of the unexpected change in performance (see Pope and Mihaljek, 1992).

Example 6.1   Forecast Bias in Project Appraisals: Example of World Bank Experience

SUMMARY STATISTICS FOR 1,015 WORLD BANK PROJECTS

	Mean	Median	Maximum	Minimum	Standard deviation
Economic rate of return (per cent)					
At appraisal	22	18	158	1	13
At project completion	16	14	128	−20	13
Total project cost (million US dollars, current prices)					
At appraisal	86	34	3,193	1	185
At project completion	102	40	4,045	1	233
Nominal cost overrun (per cent)	22	10	514	−89	46
Unexpected inflation (per cent)	20	23	38	−2	7
Real cost overrun (per cent)	−6	−11	394	−91	34
Time overrun (years)	2	2	16	−4	2
Time overrun (per cent)	58	46	405	−68	56

Note: Project completion refers to start-up of normal operations.

Source: Pope and Mihaljek (1992).

It has sometimes been suggested that governments are in a better position to deal with risk and uncertainty and that there is no need to take account explicitly of risk and uncertainty in public sector project evaluations. This argument may be based in part on a belief that some of the risks and uncertainties facing a specific project may be within governmental control and should therefore not be explicitly dealt with. It could also be argued that because of the size of national or EU investment programmes there is inevitably a degree of risk pooling, which should have an impact on the treatment of risks for a specific public sector project. Governments and markets are both in a good position to pool resources, but one is still left with the covariance risk, i.e. that part of the risk that is correlated with risk in the economy as a whole.

The author believes that despite the existence of risk pooling it would be very foolish to ignore the issue of risk and uncertainty associated with EU or other public sector projects. To do so would be to bias investments towards projects with a more risky or less certain outcome. Such an approach also opens up the possibility of a distortion between public and private sector projects. This would result in overinvestment of EU or exchequer-funded projects, with commercial projects being crowded out and a resultant misallocation of resources.

6.2 ALTERNATIVE APPROACHES

If it is accepted that the issue of risk and uncertainty must be taken into account in the evaluation of EU structural funds and other public sector investments, the question arises of what are the approaches that can in practice be used to handle risk as broadly defined. As many individual project or programme evaluations fail to deal adequately with this issue, it is useful to consider alternative approaches in some detail. The following table presents possible approaches to the treatment of risk or uncertainty in project evaluations.

Approaches to the Treatment of Risk
• Research on key demand and cost variables • Reduction in annual net benefits • Reduction in assumed life span • Increase in discount rate • Scenario analysis • Sensitivity analysis • Statistical simulation • Estimation of probabilities • Use of pay-back as well as NPV estimates in decision-making • Threshold analysis

Research on Key Demand and Cost Variables

The most useful approach to the treatment of risk is to ensure that the base case assumptions for the key demand and cost variables are adequately researched. The level of resources given to the evaluation of demand and capital costs in public sector investment appraisals should be at least as good as would be undertaken by commercial investors. Too often key estimates are based on assumptions rather than on comprehensive research. It is argued elsewhere in this book that the quality of the input data used in the investment or programme evaluations must be given as much or more attention as is given to the development of sophisticated models or to technical economic assumptions. This may require the input of a multidisciplinary team. Some of the issues as well as the methods that can be used to estimate demand and capital costs are discussed in chapter 7.

Reduction in Annual Net Benefits

One approach to the treatment of risk and uncertainty is to simply reduce the annual net benefits, either by increasing the capital cost estimates or by taking what is sometimes referred to as a conservative view on annual benefits. While this approach is to some extent arbitrary, it has the advantage of simplicity. The judgment of an experienced analyst on which assumptions should be framed in more conservative form and by what amount can in practice often be a very good guide to realistic project evaluation. The problem with this approach relates to the dependence on the analyst's judgment. This is, however, only one of many areas of investment appraisal where judgment will be relevant, and it would be a mistake to assume that this factor can be removed from such appraisals.

Reduction in Assumed Life Span

An alternative approach to the handling of risk in investment evaluations is to reduce the assumed life span of the project. This has the impact of reducing the net benefits. Often the expected physical life of a capital infrastructure investment can be very long, while it may be thought appropriate to restrict this to a certain period. This can be useful where the risks or uncertainties are seen as increasing over time. For example, unforeseen technological developments may make some infrastructure redundant in the future, even if the physical aspects of the infrastructure remain intact. Similarly, it is increasingly difficult to forecast demand or market conditions beyond a certain period. The risks or uncertainty that the benefits may not continue beyond a certain period suggest that, even where engineering estimates indicate that an infrastructure or investment may have a technically useful life of a specified number of years, it may be appropriate to reduce this assumed life span to take account of risks or uncertainties. In considering the impact of any such reduction, the influence of the discount rate used in reducing benefits beyond a certain period should be considered.

In practice, reducing the assumed life span of a project can be a useful approach to handling risk and uncertainty. This must, however, be handled with care, as it could have the effect of biasing investments towards projects with short-term rather than long-term impacts.

Increase in Discount Rate

The issues arising in the choice of a discount rate were discussed in chapter 5. The analysis suggested that the main purpose of a discount rate was to take account of the cost of servicing national debt. It was also mentioned that it is sometimes suggested that the discount rate could be increased or 'loaded' to take account of risk.

Using the discount rate to adjust for risk raises a number of theoretical issues. However, of more importance is the fact that its use implicitly suggests that the risks or uncertainties are increasing with time on a strict compounding basis. The use of the discount rate to take account of risk (if applied as a single rate in a project evaluation) assumes the same level of risk or uncertainty for each of the components of costs and benefits and, as indicated above, assumes that these increase with time in a precise manner.

The use of a higher discount rate to take account of risks creates a problem in evaluating on a comparative basis a number of investment programmes undertaken by different analysts. This issue is faced by the EU or national policy-makers, as the choice is often one of deciding on the merits of competing opportunities for investment. The extent to which a higher discount rate used reflected an analyst's estimate of risk or simply a different view of the opportunity cost of capital would need to be established. A further problem with using a higher discount rate for risk is that if the risks were not increasing on a compound basis over time, then the use of an increased discount rate could inappropriately bias investments in certain directions (for example against long-term projects). The use of a higher discount rate to accommodate risk is not seen by the author as the best way to handle risk.

Scenario Analysis

Some of the risks or uncertainties associated with a programme or project may relate to different possibilities concerning the external environment. Different assumptions on the background to a project or, in other words, different possibilities for the state of the external environment or 'state of the world' can represent the risk or uncertainty for the project. This can usefully be modelled by means of scenario analysis, which involves examining the effects of a number of different scenarios. These risks or uncertainties are not project-specific but can have a direct impact on project or programme outcomes. The choice of scenarios will depend on the particular circumstances of the investment. They could, for example, involve examining the impact of changes in overall economic growth forecasts, or the emergence of international overcapacity in a sector, or volatility in exchange rates, and so on.

Scenario analysis can be of use in specific cases where a project or programme's outcome is significantly influenced directly by changes in the external environment. Such an analysis can assist policy-makers in identifying the impact of alternative scenarios or outcomes on the merits of the project.

Sensitivity Analysis

A concept related to scenario analysis is sensitivity analysis. This technique enables one to examine the sensitivity of the outcome of an investment or programme appraisal to changes in key assumptions or variables.

Sensitivity analysis is particularly useful where the degree of risk or uncertainty for selected variables is unknown. By adjusting the variables that comprise the costs or benefits of a project one can establish the importance of these variables or assumptions. A sensitivity analysis is therefore a technique that assists in the evaluating of risks as broadly defined by revising projections for specified assumptions. This enables one to ascertain how the revisions affect the estimated economic (or financial) results of the investment or programme.

Sensitivity analysis can be particularly useful in identifying the risks or uncertainty to the base case findings and the source of the risks or uncertainties. For example, it may emerge that a major change in the assumed value of some variable may have little impact on the merits of the project. In such cases changes in this variable are unlikely to be relevant to the project appraisal. In contrast, it may emerge that even small changes to some other variable could have an effect on the project's economic viability. Clearly in that case a lot of attention is required on the robustness of the initial estimate. If policy-makers are informed by a sensitivity analysis of the consequences of the most likely outcomes, this can be an invaluable tool for effective project evaluation.

The two key issues that should be tackled in sensitivity analysis are ensuring that the sensitivity of all key variables is examined and ensuring that reasonable assumptions are made concerning the extent to which the variables are varied. Empirical research on previous experience can be very useful in this task.

While sensitivity analysis can be used to examine the impact of changes on the likely outcomes for all the variables where there is uncertainty, it is usually necessary, for practical purposes, to confine the detailed analysis to key variables. As part of the working papers associated with an investment appraisal it may be appropriate to 'run' a large number of sensitivities in order to isolate the major sources of risk or uncertainty that would significantly affect the outcome of the appraisal.

In completing a sensitivity analysis it is usual practice to consider a more favourable assumption as well as a less favourable assumption for the key variables. It is, however, important that the nature and purpose of a sensitivity analysis is understood and that it is not seen as an *à la carte* or 'pick your own choice' approach, which would enable the promoters of a project to choose all the favourable assumptions to justify an investment. Sensitivities should be presented as variations on the base case; this should represent the outcome that is thought most likely to occur. In some cases it may be important to consider a combination of unfavourable assumptions and not simply to isolate the sensitivity of the project's results on a variable-by-variable basis.

Statistical Simulation

Statistical simulation is another approach that can be used to handle risk or uncertainty in the evaluation of public sector investments. Statistical simulation is used in the commercial sector where major capital expenditures are involved. It is in essence a more detailed and sophisticated form of sensitivity analysis, which can widen the practical range of sensitivities examined and can present the information in the form of a number of statistical summaries and ratios. Except in very large or complex investment decisions, it is probably not necessary. Statistical simulation can also assist in the estimation of probabilities.

Estimation of Probabilities

A potentially useful (but seldom used) approach for dealing with risk is the estimation of probabilities for the key variables where risks are attached. The identification of these variables can often be provided by the use of sensitivity analysis or statistical simulation. The estimation of probability is usually more relevant for very large and comprehensive evaluations. If a risk attaches to a particular variable or outcome, it is important to attempt to evaluate the range of likely outcomes associated with this variable and whether the probability of these outcomes can be evaluated. The attachment of probabilities or expected or likely values to possible outcomes is one of the best ways of approaching risk. The weighting of the likelihood of possible outcomes is the basis for setting insurance premiums in the commercial sector; similar approaches can be applied in evaluating public sector investments. The estimation of probabilities involves estimating the range of likely outcomes for key variables and estimating the likelihood of values occurring within the range identified. Risk can therefore be accommodated formally in a project appraisal by the aggregation or summation of probabilities.

In practice, there are a number of different ways of assigning probabilities, which will in part be dictated by the level of information available. One approach is to assign a probability value based on an empirical review of previous experience. For example, if past evidence indicates that 20 per cent of industrial development projects fail within a certain period, or if 70 per cent of tourists do not make return visits, this could be used to assign probabilities to these aspects in evaluating new projects or programmes.

More formal techniques can also be used to estimate probabilities, such as the Monte Carlo technique. This involves developing a data-base on similar projects and computing the value of variables on a repetitive basis, which, following statistical analysis, can produce a set of probability weights.

A less rigorous approach would be to choose from a range of classic probability distributions the one that in the experience of the analyst best fits the particular variable. While unsatisfactory in a number of respects, this approach can be useful in summarising or in presenting a judgment of the range of risks involved.

Use of Pay-Back As Well As NPV in Decision-Making

The pay-back technique considers the number of years it is expected to take before the net income or net benefit 'pay-back' of the initial investment is achieved. As indicated in chapter 2, this technique suffers from the fundamental problem that it takes no account of the costs and benefits that arise after the specified period for the pay-back.

Despite these problems, the use of the pay-back technique may in certain cases be of benefit as a rough-and-ready rule of thumb for handling risk and uncertainty in project or programme evaluations. This should be used, however, only in combination with net present value measures and only as part of the judgment on the risks or uncertainties involved. In many ways this technique is very similar to the approach of reducing the assumed life span of a project as a way of handling risk, as discussed above. The use of a pay-back estimate may be of value if there is a possibility of a sudden and significant decline in benefits or a sudden escalation in costs. It could, for example, be useful in circumstances where the benefits of the project depend on market conditions, which could be influenced by capacity additions or technological changes. Where there is a possibility of 'sudden death' for a project caused by such external or other factors, the speed at which the project pays back its investment is clearly of particular relevance in evaluating the likely risks.

Threshold Analysis

The threshold analysis technique as a way of approaching risk and uncertainty in project or programme appraisal is very similar to sensitivity analysis. Indeed this technique could be considered as simply a different way of presenting the sensitivity results. The threshold analysis approach considers how much variance would be necessary in one or more of the key variables of a project to affect the project's merits. This can be useful in indicating that even if major negative changes in the key variable were to occur, a project might still be justified. Similarly it can be used to show that for more marginal investments even relatively small changes in key variables could alter the merits of proceeding with the project. This approach therefore takes account of risk by indicating the threshold or line for key variables beyond which the merits of the investment are reversed.

* * *

Importance of Evaluating Risk

Risk and uncertainty are inherent in most aspects of nearly all investment or project evaluations. It is essential that they are evaluated as part of the appraisal of public sector projects as well as for commercial investment evaluations. A wide range of techniques is available for handling risk; the approach will depend on the size and the nature of the project or programme under investigation. In most cases, however, a sensitivity analysis is recommended as part of the approach to the handling of risk.

7

NON-TECHNICAL PITFALLS

Investment appraisal is an area fraught with difficulties, and at least some investments have been undertaken where negative returns could have been predicted if appropriate evaluations were completed. In evaluating investments financed by EU structural funds or other public sector projects, there are numerous additional technical pitfalls that arise, as distinct from the task of evaluating the commercial viability of investments. These issues were discussed in previous chapters and relate to factors such as inappropriate estimation of opportunity costs or discount rates. In addition to these technical issues there are a number of non-technical pitfalls that in practice can be of even greater significance. Policy-makers faced with the failure of some investments to achieve the predicted returns will in many cases realise that such circumstances were caused by non-technical pitfalls in the project assessment rather than any differences between economists on technical estimates of areas such as shadow pricing.

Two areas that can lead to the wrong choice of investment opportunities are:

- overestimation of demand
- underestimation of capital costs.

These pitfalls apply to both financial and economic investment appraisals.

7.1 OVERESTIMATION OF DEMAND

Importance of Realistic Demand Forecasts

The cornerstone of the evaluation of investments is a realistic forecast of demand for the output or use of the proposed investment. Despite the significance of this factor, which will determine the size of the estimated benefits of the investment, it is sometimes given less attention than the development of apparently sophisticated project appraisal models or the evaluation of specific technical economic or financial assumptions. A major task facing policy-makers in evaluating public sector investments is ensuring that the key basic data (on areas such as the level of forecast demand) is adequate. Poor data on the key variables makes a nonsense of sophisticated appraisal techniques.

As an investment that has no demand for its output has no benefits, the issue of forecast demand is the most fundamental question, which must be rigorously addressed in project appraisals. This applies to projects where the output is not sold in the market as well as to investments that are part of the market economy. For example, the economic benefits of investment in a public sector transport infrastructure may be primarily measured in terms of variables such as time savings or reductions in accident costs, etc. The significance of these benefits will be determined by the level of use or demand for the infrastructure. In evaluating investments where the output is sold in the market (for example airports, ports, tourism and industrial projects), the issue of the level of forecast demand is clearly of critical importance in evaluating either the financial or economic impact of the project.

Danger of Applying Long-Term Growth Rates

One particular danger is to assume the application of growth rates to demand over a long period. Even apparently relatively small real growth rates can have a major cumulative impact over a long period, the realism of which is sometimes not adequately evaluated.

Elements in Appraisal of Demand

While the specific methods that should be used in evaluating demand and the detailed areas of interest will vary significantly between different projects or programmes, an illustrative outline of the key tasks and outputs for this element of appraisal is given in chart 7.1.

The forecasting of demand in investment appraisals requires an evaluation and understanding of overall demand trends as well as a detailed analysis of the potential demand for the specific investment.

An understanding of the determinants of overall demand trends is the first requirement in the forecasting of demand for a specific project. Cyclical trends in market demand for areas where public sector investments have been undertaken (such as steel, fertilisers, oil refining, etc.) can often result

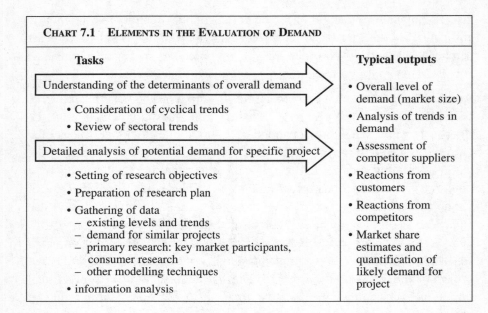

CHART 7.1   ELEMENTS IN THE EVALUATION OF DEMAND

Tasks

Understanding of the determinants of overall demand

• Consideration of cyclical trends
• Review of sectoral trends

Detailed analysis of potential demand for specific project

• Setting of research objectives
• Preparation of research plan
• Gathering of data
 – existing levels and trends
 – demand for similar projects
 – primary research: key market participants,
  consumer research
 – other modelling techniques
• information analysis

Typical outputs

• Overall level of demand (market size)
• Analysis of trends in demand
• Assessment of competitor suppliers
• Reactions from customers
• Reactions from competitors
• Market share estimates and quantification of likely demand for project

in dramatic changes to the level of forecast demand. In other areas, such as transport or tourism, changes in overall economic growth can significantly alter the estimated levels of demand. A review of sectoral trends can therefore be a critical task in investment appraisals.

In addition to reviewing the overall trends in demand it is also essential to undertake a detailed analysis of the potential demand for the specific investment. The significance of this can be seen by considering the example of an economic appraisal of a specific industrial project that fails in the market a short time after implementation. That would clearly make the economic appraisal irrelevant unless this has been considered. Similarly, a regional airport that cannot attract tourism or business traffic will fail to realise potential benefits.

As the forecasting of demand is an area that is central to project evaluations, it is useful to review some aspects of the approach to researching demand for a specific investment and also to discuss the type of areas that should be considered in this element of project evaluations. Of course, as suggested above, the appropriate approach to the forecasting of demand will vary from project to project.

Four Steps in Forecasting Demand

There are essentially four steps involved in the effective evaluation of forecast demand for an investment, namely, setting of the research objectives, preparation of the research plan, gathering of information, and information analysis.

The setting of research objectives in evaluating potential demand is the first practical step. Unless the scope of the evaluation is defined, it is likely that analysts' time and resources will be wasted or diverted into unnecessary areas. These objectives must be based on an overall plan for the investment appraisal.

The second practical step is the preparation of a research plan that would specify the information requirements necessary to evaluate demand and the most efficient way of gathering this information. This might involve the use of formal demand models, which can be very useful in evaluating investments in selected areas. For many investment proposals a more targeted research plan will be required.

The gathering of information required to forecast demand is typically one of the most time-consuming elements in investment appraisal. Where possible, use should be made of secondary data, in other words, information that is already in existence. This can include information on the existing level and trends in demand where an investment involves an expansion or replacement of an existing project. Also of potential use is the level of demand achieved by similar previous investments. It is usually necessary, particularly for larger investments, to gather information through primary data sources, in other words, information that must be collected specifically for the particular investment appraisal. Primary data is usually acquired through surveys of key market participants or experts or through consumer research. Particular care must be exercised in using certain research methods designed to forecast demand (for example stated preference techniques), and the implicit bias in some of these approaches must be taken into account. (Stated preference or contingent valuation is the technique that attempts to determine values or future demand from consumers' stated views, in contrast to the inference of demand or prices based on actual revealed consumer behaviour.)

The final and most important stage in evaluating potential demand is the information analysis. This is an area where common sense and judgment, based on the previous experience of the analyst, are likely to be more important than any specific technique.

Main Areas to Be Considered in Forecasting Demand

In forecasting demand, the type of areas to be considered will, as suggested above, need to be tailored to the specific investment under evaluation. Typically, however, this is likely to include the following elements: overall level of demand, trends in demand, assessment of competitive suppliers, reactions from customers and competitors, and quantification of likely demand for the investment.

The overall level of demand will involve a quantification of the level of demand in the area while the investment is planned. For an industrial project this could involve analysis of the international demand, while for a tourism project it might be appropriate to focus on the relevant segment of tourism demand. For transport investments it may involve a review of national or regional origin or destination traffic flows. For private sector commercial investment appraisals this is usually referred to as quantification of the total market size. The ease or difficulty in quantifying the overall level of demand will depend on the area being investigated and the level of official and other statistics available. One potential danger in defining the area of demand too widely is that very large estimates of overall demand may result, which could give a mistaken impression of the challenge in achieving even a very small share of this demand when considering a specific investment.

A second area that will usually be reviewed is the trend in demand and an understanding of the determinants of changes in the level of demand. In some cases this may be facilitated by an econometric modelling exercise, while in other cases a less formal approach may be more effective. The forecast level of demand for a specific investment project will be significantly influenced by whether overall demand is expanding or contracting.

The assessment of competitor suppliers is usually of importance in evaluating the realism of demand projections for a specific project. Competitor suppliers are defined here as the competing infrastructure as well as other companies or organisations supplying demand. Thus, for example, the road network may be a competitor supplier that should be evaluated in considering a rail investment project. Similarly, a port may represent competition to investment in an airport or a cross-border road system. More direct competition, for example between manufacturers or between two regional airport authorities, is clearly of key importance.

The reaction of competitors or consumers to an investment should also form a key part of any economic or financial investment appraisal. Feedback in this area is of importance in evaluating future demand projections.

On the basis of the above elements of research, it is necessary to quantify a realistic forecast for demand associated with an investment. The enthusiasm of the promoters can frequently result in an upward bias in the level of forecast demand and thereby the level of benefits associated with a proposed investment. This issue can, in part, be dealt with by the methods used to handle risk referred to in the previous chapter. It is essential, however, that realistic base case assumptions for demand are incorporated in all financial and economic investment appraisals. The overestimation of forecast demand is one of the most common practical pitfalls in project appraisals.

7.2 UNDERESTIMATION OF CAPITAL COSTS

In most European countries there are oft-quoted examples of dramatic increases in the capital costs of major public and private sector investments. An underestimation of the capital costs can clearly be one of the most serious errors in investment appraisals. An increase in the estimated capital costs can have a significant impact on the relevance of project appraisals.

Danger of Promoter Enthusiasm

There is also a danger that the promoters of particular projects may err on the side of an underestimation of the expected capital costs in order to ensure that the project passes the initial appraisal.

Issue of Implementation

Difficulties arise in the evaluation of capital costs as much depends not only on the initial estimates but on whether 'best practice' will be applied during the construction stages of the investment. This is something that is very difficult for an analyst to handle in evaluating a specific investment.

Comparison with Similar Projects

One approach to ensuring that capital cost estimates are realistic is to examine the actual level of costs incurred in similar projects and the extent to which there was any escalation in costs compared with the initial estimates. This is particularly useful where very similar investment projects have recently been completed. It is useful to compare capital cost estimates with expenditure based on actual tenders for similar projects (indexed for inflation where appropriate); such an approach is clearly less useful in practice where the investment is a unique project. Even in such a case, however, experience in other countries may provide some broad yardstick against which to evaluate the specific capital cost estimates.

Contingency Sums

It is essential in both economic and financial investment appraisals that a contingency sum is included in the initial capital cost estimates. Whether this should be further increased to reflect possible additional cost overruns depends on the range of cost escalations, if any, generally experienced for public sector investments in the member-state in which the project is being undertaken. Occasional reviews of this by policy-makers could provide some general guidance for individual investment appraisals.

In the absence of any information on this area, an assumption of a minimum real 5 per cent increase in the capital costs may be appropriate for project appraisal purposes (of course from the perspective of project implementation for approved investments any cost escalation could be seen as unacceptable). It is also essential to ensure that realistic assessments of the phasing of capital expenditures are made. In project management rather than project appraisal (which is the subject of this book) the issue of the credibility and enforceability of contracts, including price adjustment clauses, is important.

Treatment of Inflation

The treatment of inflation in capital cost estimates also requires attention. While economic project appraisals should be undertaken in real terms, if a different inflation rate is likely for capital costs compared with projected benefits this needs to be taken into account.

Timing of Decision

The problem of estimating capital costs for inclusion in public sector investment projects is made more difficult by the fact that at the stage of the investment appraisal, detailed design information is usually not available, and it is only when this is prepared that authoritative cost estimates can be formulated. Even at this much later stage in a project, cost escalations can emerge because of specific construction problems, misjudgments on likely tender prices, or mismanagement during implementation of the project.

As a result of these factors it is essential that where possible the final decision on whether to proceed with an investment project takes place not at the investment appraisal stage but only after tender prices for capital costs are obtained. This applies even when some costs have already been incurred. Indeed it is critical that there is a procedure for authorising capital expenditure at each stage of a project; and while this is not part of investment appraisal as such, it is a requirement for ensuring the best use of resources. It may be useful as part of the investment appraisal to indicate the level of increase in capital costs that would undermine the justification for the investment.

8

PRACTICAL STEPS IN APPRAISAL

8.1 Overview of Elements in Appraisal

This chapter considers the practical steps that are relevant in the appraisal of EU structural funds and other public sector investments or programmes. These will of course vary depending on the nature of the evaluation to be completed, but most of the steps identified will be applicable to many evaluations, and all the steps are likely to be necessary in evaluating the merits of major capital investment projects.

The main elements in the appraisal of public sector programmes or investments are summarised in the following table. Many of the elements are related and in practice will be undertaken simultaneously. The order in which the different elements will be undertaken may also vary.

Elements in appraisal
<ul><li>Clarification of issues</li><li>Definition of objectives of appraisal</li><li>Choice of method for appraisal</li><li>Consideration of strategic issues</li><li>Development of detailed work programme</li></ul>

Clarification of the Issues

The first task in the appraisal is to clarify the problems or issues that are to be addressed; in other words, this concerns consideration of why the appraisal is being undertaken.

Definition of Objectives

Once the key issues of concern have been clarified, it is then possible to define the objectives of the appraisal precisely. These should be set out in as comprehensive a manner as possible and should be clearly defined. Care should be taken in the formulation of the objectives of the appraisal, as this will determine future steps in the evaluation.

Choice of Method

It is only when the objectives of the appraisal are precisely defined that an informed choice of the appropriate method for the appraisal can be established. There is a danger that policy-makers and economists will identify a method on the basis of a specific approach that they understand and have experience of rather than by considering the appropriate method for addressing the specific objectives of the appraisal. It is necessary that the analysts undertaking the appraisal should consider a range of options and recommend the approach best suited to the issues of concern. This may involve a number of different approaches.

In chapter 1, four main methods for evaluating public sector projects were identified, as follows:

- Strategic reviews
- Cost-effectiveness studies
- Financial appraisals
- Cost-benefit analysis

In the special circumstances where the scale of the investment programme is sufficiently large, macro-economic evaluations may be relevant.

Each of these approaches has a contribution to make, and their applicability will vary depending on the specific objectives of the appraisal. In chart 8.1 some of the strengths and areas of applicability of each of these approaches are summarised.

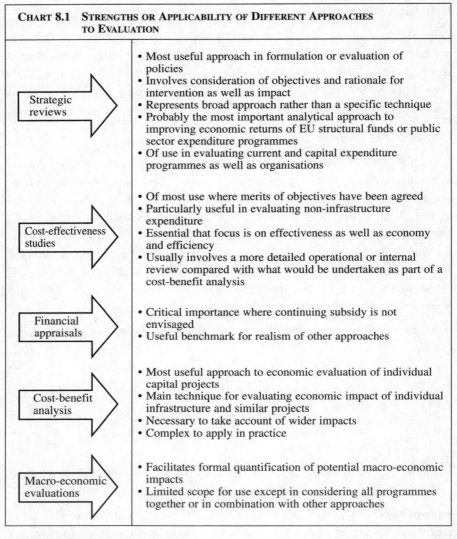

CHART 8.1   STRENGTHS OR APPLICABILITY OF DIFFERENT APPROACHES TO EVALUATION

Strategic reviews
- Most useful approach in formulation or evaluation of policies
- Involves consideration of objectives and rationale for intervention as well as impact
- Represents broad approach rather than a specific technique
- Probably the most important analytical approach to improving economic returns of EU structural funds or public sector expenditure programmes
- Of use in evaluating current and capital expenditure programmes as well as organisations

Cost-effectiveness studies
- Of most use where merits of objectives have been agreed
- Particularly useful in evaluating non-infrastructure expenditure
- Essential that focus is on effectiveness as well as economy and efficiency
- Usually involves a more detailed operational or internal review compared with what would be undertaken as part of a cost-benefit analysis

Financial appraisals
- Critical importance where continuing subsidy is not envisaged
- Useful benchmark for realism of other approaches

Cost-benefit analysis
- Most useful approach to economic evaluation of individual capital projects
- Main technique for evaluating economic impact of individual infrastructure and similar projects
- Necessary to take account of wider impacts
- Complex to apply in practice

Macro-economic evaluations
- Facilitates formal quantification of potential macro-economic impacts
- Limited scope for use except in considering all programmes together or in combination with other approaches

Consideration of Strategic Issues

Regardless of which approach is used, it is essential to consider even in summary form some of the strategic economy-wide implications of the investment or programme. This can be accommodated within a number of the specific methods identified; but even where this is not the case some preliminary consideration of the strategic context for the investment or programme will be required.

CHART 8.2 MAIN ELEMENTS IN IMPLEMENTATION OF DIFFERENT METHODOLOGIES

	External review	**Internal review**		**Development and implementation of strategy**
Strategic Reviews	• Economic environment • Sectoral structure • Competitive position/industry analysis	• Analysis of objectives • Review of current strategies • Rationale for public sector intervention • Examination of comparative approaches		• Development/ evaluation of strategy • Analysis of resource allocation and priorities • Implementation: structures, systems, and organisation • Continuous review
	Review of objectives	**Evaluation of economy efficiency**	**Evaluation of effectiveness**	**Development of conclusions**
Cost Effective-ness Studies	• Preliminary assessment of coherence of objectives	• Review of current practice • Consideration of alternative approaches • Use of comparative statistics/ benchmarking • Cost measures • Productivity measures	• Review of performance/ experience • Analysis of performance measures • GAP analysis • Comparative reviews • Views of policy-makers • Market research • Case histories • Time series analysis	• Evaluation of effectiveness • 'With' and 'without' analysis
	Identification of option for evaluation	**Projection of costs and benefits**	**Adjustment for risk and time**	**Analysis and decision**
Financial Appraisals	• Range of options • Specific investment examination	• Identification • Valuation	• Treatment of risk • Discounting	• NPV calculations • Other key ratios
Cost-Benefit Analysis	• Range of options • Specific investment examination	• Identification • Valuation	• Treatment of risk • Discounting	• NPV calculations • Other key ratios
	Review of economic policies	**Development of benchmark projections**		**Evaluation of macro-impact**
Macro-Economic Evalua-tions	• Overall context for initial projections • Consideration of external impacts • High-level review of potential impacts of programme	• Taking account of international economic development • Projections on GDP, unemployment, and external trade		• Identification of key programme impacts • Consideration of overall impact on projection • Comparison of modified projections with initial benchmark projects

Development of Work Programme

All properly managed project evaluations should be based on a detailed work programme. What is relevant here is not so much sophisticated presentation material and flow charts (which in any case usually require significant modification as an appraisal proceeds) but rather a clear understanding of the specific tasks required as part of the implementation of the method chosen. These can only be identified on a project-by-project basis, but the main areas involved in each of the methods listed above are presented in chart 8.2. This shows that the same issues are addressed in both financial and economic appraisal methods. The differences arise at a more detailed level. In particular, they arise in relation to how the costs and benefits are valued. The subsequent steps in appraisal discussed in this chapter are applicable mainly to cost-benefit analysis and also to financial appraisal, except that in the latter the valuation of benefits and costs is more straightforward.

The focus in this chapter on these two methods is because the techniques for these approaches are fairly standard and merit discussion. The other two main approaches of strategic reviews and cost-effectiveness studies are less standard and must be designed on a case-by-case basis.

8.2 STEPS IN COST-BENEFIT ANALYSIS AND FINANCIAL APPRAISALS

The main elements in cost-benefit analysis and in financial appraisals are as follows:

Main Steps in Cost-Benefit Analysis
• Identification of options for evaluation
• Identification of likely areas of costs and benefits
• Decision on project period for examination
• Evaluation of benefits in monetary terms
• Evaluation of costs in monetary terms
• Discounting of costs and benefits

Main Steps in Cost-Benefit Analysis – *continued*

- Identification of costs and benefits not amenable to monetary quantification

- Decision on how to handle risk and uncertainty

- Specification of assessment criteria

- Interpretation and analysis of findings

- Development of conclusions and, where appropriate, recommendations

---

Identification of options

A key issue in project or programme appraisal is the choice of the options for evaluation. In principle all options should be considered, including a 'do minimum' or a 'do nothing' option. In practice there is a need to limit the number of options that can be considered. In the case of projects already in existence the 'do nothing' option may involve the continuation of existing operations versus new investment, but it may also be appropriate in certain cases to include a closure option. In some cases, however, this option may not be appropriate, because of the impacts outside the project. For example, in considering the upgrading of a road investment, closure of the road may be less costly than a 'do minimum' or upgrading, but this may not be a sensible option.

What is critical, however, is that policy-makers understand and agree on the options and that the basis for the appraisals are clearly understood. The choice of options for appraisal should reflect a clear understanding of what the realistic choices are. This requires clarity in framing the objectives of the appraisal, as discussed above.

Even where it is agreed by policy-makers that some options should be excluded from the analysis, this should usually be made explicit, and where possible there should be a reference to any possible consequences of the choice of options decided. It is important to realise that cost-benefit analysis, financial appraisal or any other techniques are simply tools for analysis, and there can be no definitive rules on the range of options for evaluation. However, as indicated above, only in exceptional cases should the 'do nothing' or 'do minimum' option be excluded, and in general any options that are excluded should be made explicit. This is particularly important in ensuring that the findings are not misrepresented.

Identification of Costs and Benefits

It is appropriate at an early stage of an economic cost-benefit or financial appraisal to identify all the likely areas of costs or benefits. This is particularly important in ensuring that in the subsequent measurement of costs and benefits none are overlooked. Care should be taken to ensure that all relevant capital and operating costs as well as all benefits are included.

For certain types of evaluation it may be necessary to specify costs and benefits using a particular structure. The following table presents a summary of the information required to be supplied to the European Commission as part of the Structural Funds Regulations.

Information Required by the European Commission on Structural Fund Projects

INFORMATION CONCERNING A MAJOR PROJECT FOR INFRASTRUCTURE INVESTMENT COSTING MORE THAN 25 MILLION ECU

SOCIO-ECONOMIC COST-BENEFIT ANALYSIS

- Socio-economic cost-benefit analysis covering
  - costs and benefits during project implementation
  - income and management costs during the operational phase
  - direct benefits for users of the infrastructure
  - indirect benefits for the regional economy stemming from the infrastructure
  - diseconomies created by the infrastructure
  - foreseeable rate of utilisation
  - overall assessment of the socio-economic costs and benefits of the project
  - estimated impact of changes in the parameters on the results of the analysis

---

- Internal economic rate of return
- If the infrastructure is to be fully or partially managed according to commercial criteria, the financial rate of return

Foreseeable impact on development and conversion of the region

- Jobs directly created during project implementation: number and duration
- Number of jobs directly created during the operational phase of the infrastructure
- Number of jobs indirectly created (induced)
- Extent to which the region is at present endowed with the type of infrastructure proposed, compared with requirements
- Main beneficiaries of the infrastructure
- Permanent effects of the infrastructure on the region's economic performance (GDP etc.) and its contribution to exploiting the region's development potential

Impact of EU assistance on project implementation

- Will assistance
  - accelerate implementation of the project?
  - be essential to implementation of the project?
  - form an integral part of the financing plan?
  - make for an increase in the amount of public expenditure on the project?

INFORMATION CONCERNING A MAJOR PROJECT FOR PRODUCTIVE INVESTMENT COSTING MORE THAN 15 MILLION ECU

Situation of the market in the sector concerned

- Situation of the sector and expected evolution; information on supply and demand on the market(s), broken down, where appropriate, by member-state and region on the one hand and third countries, considered as a whole, on the other hand
- References and conclusions of market analyses and sectoral studies

Direct and indirect impact of the investment on employment
- Number of permanent jobs before the investment
- Number of jobs needed by the investment
- Number of jobs that would be lost if the investment is not realised
- Jobs created during the implementation of the investment: number and average duration
- Estimation of jobs indirectly created in the region

Analysis of expected profitability
- Results of appropriate profitability assessment:
  - costs of investment
  - expected operating results and hypothesis on which this expectation is based (evolution of the market, revenues, costs of production)
  - calculation of the profitability rate
  - estimate of the sensitivity of the results of the analysis to changes in the parameters
- Period of reference (time horizon taken into consideration in the calculation of profitability)
- Estimated increase in annual value added realised by the enterprise as a result of the investment
- Induced effects of the investment on the regional economy

Valuation of Costs and Benefits in Monetary Terms

Practical steps in project evaluations involve deciding on the period for examination and valuation of the costs and benefits in monetary terms. In principle the project period for examination should reflect the likely useful economic life of the options under review. It is important that the period for analysis (which will form the basis for net present value estimates) is based on economically useful life and not simply on the estimated technical life of the assets. As indicated in chapter 6, the project period is sometimes adjusted to take account of risk or uncertainty; however, there are dangers in such adjustments.

The valuation of benefits in monetary terms is one of the most difficult and critical aspects of investment or other appraisals. This will, in nearly all cases, involve an assessment of forecast demand. Some of the typical elements in this task are outlined below.

Elements in demand evaluation

Understanding of the determinants of overall demand trends

- Consideration of cyclical trends
- Review of sectoral trends

Detailed analysis of potential demand for specific project

- Setting of research objectives
- Preparation of research plan
- Gathering of data
  - Existing levels and trends
  - Demand for similar projects
  - Primary research: key market participants, consumer research
  - Other modelling techniques
- Information analysis

The valuation of the benefits of economic cost-benefit studies is more complex than in the case of financial or commercial appraisals. This will involve the use of shadow prices, as discussed in earlier chapters.

One of the main reasons why projects fail to achieve expected economic or financial returns is the failure to achieve demand projections. The other main cause is an underestimation of costs, particularly capital costs. A key element in a financial or economic appraisal is the correct estimation of costs in monetary terms.

In economic cost-benefit studies, costs need to be valued in terms of the economic or social costs, and this adds further complexity to the assessment.

Discounting

When the costs and benefits of the project or programme have been quantified in monetary terms, it is necessary to discount these flows to ensure comparability of costs and benefits that occur at different periods. Discounting can also be used in economic project evaluations to reflect the social or opportunity cost of capital or in practice to reflect the alternative use of the funds in terms of repayment of national debt.

In discounting costs and benefits, care must be taken in the choice of the discount rate. In relation to economic appraisals it is necessary to present the figures in constant prices before discounting. Where different price increases are likely to apply to components of costs or benefits, this needs to be incorporated in the adjustments.

Identification of Costs and Benefits Not Amenable to Monetary Quantification

An important element of project or programme evaluation is the identification of any of the costs or benefits that are not amenable to monetary quantification and therefore not included in the formal cost-benefit valuation. In general an attempt should be made to develop methods of valuing costs and benefits in monetary terms, even where no immediate money value is available. In certain areas, however, this may not be possible. In these circumstances an attempt should be made to quantify the extent of these costs and benefits using measurements of activity, etc.

Decision on How to Handle Risk and Uncertainty

As indicated in chapter 6, one of the main issues that must be addressed in evaluating EU or public sector projects or programmes (or commercial investments) is how to handle risk. There is a wide range of approaches that can be used, including the following:

- Research on key demand and cost variables
- Reduction in annual net benefits
- Reduction in assumed life span

- Increase in discount rate
- Scenario analysis
- Statistical simulation
- Estimation of probabilities
- Use of pay-back as well as NPV estimates
- Threshold analysis

Specification of Assessment Criteria

The specification and use of assessment criteria is an integral part of any economic or financial investment or programme evaluation. In general, the most appropriate criterion is the discounted net present value (NPV) calculation.

Interpretation and Analysis of Findings

The interpretation and analysis of the findings is one of the most important elements in appraisal. This is an area where the judgment of the analyst or consultant is critical.

Develop Conclusions and, Where Appropriate, Recommendations

The final task in a project or programme evaluation is to formulate clear conclusions based on the analysis of the findings. Where appropriate, it may also be necessary to develop recommendations.

* * *

The evaluation of EU structural funds or other public sector investments is a difficult and complex task where few short-cuts are possible. Detailed research and judgments based on an objective analysis of findings on a project or programme basis are essential if the potential benefits of these expenditures are to be secured.

BIBLIOGRAPHY

Arrow, K. and Lind, R., 'Uncertainty and the evaluation of public investment decisions', *American Economic Review,* vol. 60 (1970), no. 3.

Atkinson, A. and Stiglitz, J., *Lectures on Public Economics,* New York: McGraw-Hill 1980.

Auerbach, A. and Feldstein, M. (eds.), *Handbook of Public Economics,* vol. 2, Amsterdam: North Holland 1987.

Barrett, S. and Mooney, D., 'The Naas motorway by-pass: a cost benefit analysis', *ESRI Quarterly Economic Commentary,* Jan. 1984.

Barrett, S. and Walsh, B., 'The "user pays" principle: theory and applications', in J. Blackwell and F. Convery (eds.), *Promise and Performance: Irish Environmental Policies Analysed,* Dublin: Resource and Environmental Policy Centre, University College, 1983.

Beedles, W. 'A note on evaluating non-simple investments', *Journal of Financial and Quantitative Analysis* (1978), 173–6.

Beesley, M. and Foster, C., 'The Victoria Line: social benefit and finances', *Journal of the Royal Statistical Society,* series A, vol. 128 (1965), 67–88.

Bennathan, E. and Walters, A., *Port Pricing and Investment Policy for Developing Countries,* New York: Oxford University Press 1979.

Bessieres, F. 'The "Investment 85" model of Électricité de France', *Management Science,* vol. 17 (1970), no. 4.

Bierman H. and Smidt, S., *The Capital Budgeting Decision* (7th ed.), New York: Macmillan 1988.

Blackwell, J. 'Efficiency and effectiveness in public investment appraisal', in T. Hardiman and M. Mulreany (eds.), *Efficiency and Effectiveness in the Public Domain,* Dublin: Institute of Public Administration 1991.

Blackwell, J., Convery, F., Walsh, B. and Walsh, M., *Natural Resource Allocation and State Enterprise: NET as a Case Study* (Policy Series, no. 1), Dublin: Resource and Environmental Policy Centre, University College, 1983.

Boadway, R. 'The welfare foundations of cost-benefit analysis', *Economic Journal,* vol. 84 (1974), no. 336.

Braeutigam, R. and Noel, R., 'The regulation of surface freight transportation: the welfare effects revisited', *Review of Economics and Statistics,* vol. 66 (1984), 80–87.

Brealey, R. and Myers, S., *Principles of Corporate Finance* (3rd ed.), New York: McGraw-Hill 1988.

Brewer, D. and Burt, O., 'Estimation of net social benefits from outdoor recreation', *Econometrica,* vol. 39 (1971), no. 5.

Commission on the Third London Airport, *Papers and Proceedings,* vol. 7, parts 1 and 2, London: HMSO 1970.

Conley, B., 'The value of human life in the demand for safety', *American Economic Review* (1976).

Currie, J., Murphy, J. and Schmitz, A., 'The concept of economic surplus and its use in economic analysis', *Economic Journal* (1971).

Dardis, R., 'The value of life: new evidence from the marketplace', *American Economic Review* (1980).

Department of Industry and Commerce, 'Evaluation of Export Credit Insurance and Finance Schemes' (press release), Dublin, Nov. 1991.

Department of Transport, *Central London Rail Study: a Report on Further Work,* London: HMSO 1990.

Department of Transport, *COBA 9 Manual,* London: HMSO 1985.

Desai, M. and Mazundar, D., 'A test of the hypothesis of disguised unemployment', *Economica,* Feb. 1970.

Dewhurst, R., *Business Cost Benefit Analysis,* New York: McGraw-Hill 1972.

Dorfman, R., 'The meaning of the internal rate of return', *Journal of Finance* (1981), 1010–23.

Dreze, J. and Stern, N., 'The theory of cost-benefit analysis', in A. Auerbach and M. Feldstein (eds.), *Handbook of Public Economics,* vol. 2, Amsterdam: North Holland 1987.

Epstein, L. and Turnbull, S., 'Capital asset prices and the temporal resolution of uncertainty', *Journal of Finance* (1980), 627–43.

Fama, E., 'Risk adjusted discount rates and capital budgeting under certainty', *Journal of Financial Economics* (1977), 1–24.

Feldstein, M. and Flemming, J., 'The problem of time stream evaluation: present value versus internal rate of return rules', *Bulletin of the Oxford University Institute of Statistics,* Feb. 1964.

Flowerdew, A., *Choosing a Site for the Third London Airport: the Roskill Commission's Approach: Cost-Benefit Analysis,* London: Penguin 1972.

Foster, C. and Beesley, M., 'Estimating the social benefit of constructing an underground railway in London', *Journal of the Royal Statistical Society,* series A, vol. 126 (1963), 46–78.

Gandolfi, A., 'Inflation, taxes and interest rates', *Journal of Finance* (1982), 797–807.

Gitman, L. and Mercurio, V., 'Cost of capital techniques used by major US firms: survey and analysis of "Fortune's" 1,000', *Financial Management,* winter 1982, 21–9.

Goodin, R., 'Discounting discounting', *Journal of Public Policy,* vol. 2 (1982).

Gordon, L. 'Benefit-cost analysis and resource allocation decisions', *Accounting and Organizations and Society,* vol. 14 (1989), 247–58.

Gordon, L. and Pinches, G., *Improving Capital Budgeting: a Decision Support System Approach,* Reading (Massachusetts): Addison-Wesley 1984.

Gramlich, E., *Benefit Cost Analysis of Government Programs,* Englewood Cliffs (New Jersey): Prentice-Hall 1981.

Greenfield, R., Randall, M. and Woods, J., 'Financial leverage and the use of the net present value investment criterion', *Financial Management,* autumn 1983, 20–44.

Harberger, A., 'On measuring the social opportunity cost of labour', *International Labour Review,* Jun. 1971.

Hausman, J., 'Exact consumer's surplus and deadweight loss', *American Economic Review,* vol. 71 (1981), no. 4.

Haveman, R. and Margolis, J. (eds.), *Public Expenditure and Policy Analysis* (2nd ed.), Chicago: Rand-McNally 1977.

Heady, C., 'Shadow wages and induced migration, *Oxford Economic Papers,* vol. 33 (1981), no. 1.

Hensher, D., *Review of Studies Leading to Existing Values of Travel Time, Valuation of Travel Time: Special Report,* Washington: Transportation Research Board 1976.

Hicks, J., 'Foundations of welfare economics', *Economic Journal,* Dec. 1939.

Hirschleifer, J., de Haven, J. and Milliman, J., *Water Supply: Economics, Technology and Policy,* Chicago: University of Chicago Press 1960.

HM Treasury, *Economic Appraisal in Central Government: a Technical Guide for Government Departments,* London: HMSO 1991.

HM Treasury, 'Expenditure appraisal in central government', *Treasury Bulletin,* vol. 2 (1990–91), issue 1.

HM Treasury Central Computing and Telecommunications Agency, *Appraising Investment in Information Systems: Examining the Options* (Information Systems Guide B4), Chichester: Wiley 1989.

Hoehm, J. and Randall, A., 'Too many proposals pass the benefit cost test', *American Economic Review,* vol. 79 (1989), 545–51.

Hof, J. and Rideout, D., 'Limitation of the with and without principle in benefit-cost analysis', *Public Finance Quarterly,* vol. 17 (1989), no. 2.

Honohan, P., 'Traps in appraising public projects', *Irish Banking Review,* spring 1986, 28–35.

Johnson, T., 'Returns from investment in human capital', *American Economic Review,* vol. 60 (1970), no. 4.

Just, R., Hueth, D. and Schmitz, A., *Applied Welfare Economics and Public Policy,* Englewood Cliffs (New Jersey): Prentice-Hall 1982.

Kabus, I., 'You can bank on uncertainty', *Harvard Business Review,* May–Jun. 1976, 95–105.

Kahneman, D. and Tversky, A., 'Prospect theory: an analysis of decision under risk', *Econometrica,* vol. 47 (1979), 263–91.

Kain, J., 'The use of straw men in the economic evaluation of rail transport projects', *AEA Papers and Proceedings* (1992), 487–93.

Kaldor, N., 'Welfare propositions of economic and interpersonal comparisons of utility', *Economic Journal,* Sep. 1939.

Keane, S., 'The internal rate of return and the reinvestment fallacy', *Journal of Accounting and Business Studies,* Jun. 1979, 48–55.

Kesling, G., 'Project analysis by computer simulation', *Journal of System Management,* Mar. 1970, 14–19.

Kim, S. and Farragher, E., 'Current capital budgeting practices', *Management Accounting,* Jun. 1981, 26–30.

Knight, F., *Risk, Uncertainty and Profit,* New York 1921.

Lal, D., *Methods of Project Analysis: a Review,* Baltimore (Maryland): Johns Hopkins University Press 1974.

Levy, H. and Sarnat, M., *Capital Investment and Financial Decisions* (4th ed.), Englewood Cliffs (New Jersey): Prentice-Hall 1989.

Lewellen, W., Lanser, H. and McConnell, J., 'Payback substitutes for discounted cash flow', *Financial Management,* summer 1973, 17–25.

Little, I. and Mirrlees, J., *Manual of Industrial Project Analysis in Developing Countries, Vol. 2: Social Cost-Benefit Analysis,* Paris: OECD 1969.

McKeon, J., 'The economic appraisal of industrial projects in Ireland', *Journal of the Statistical and Social Inquiry Society of Ireland,* vol. 24 (1979–80), 119–43.

McMahon, J., 'The IDA's Economic Appraisal System' (paper presented to Industrial Studies Association), Dublin 1985.

Magee, J., 'How to use decision trees in capital investment', *Harvard Business Review,* Sep.–Oct. 1964, 79–96.

Mansergh, N., 'The value of cost-benefit analysis of road projects', *ESRI Quarterly Economic Commentary,* Apr. 1985.

Marchand, M., 'The economic principles of telephone rates under a budgetary constraint', *Review of Economic Studies,* vol. 40 (1973), no. 124.

Mishan, E., *Cost-Benefit Analysis* (4th ed.), London: Allen and Unwin 1988.

Mishan, E., 'The new controversy about the rationale of economic evaluation', *Journal of Economic Issues,* vol. 16 (1982), no. 1.

Myers, S., 'Interactions of corporate financing and investment decisions: implications for capital budgeting', *Journal of Finance,* Mar. 1974, 1–25.

Olson, M. and Bailey, M., 'Positive time preference', *Journal of Political Economy*, Feb. 1981.

Overseas Development Administration, *Appraisal of Projects in Developing Countries: a Guide for Economists,* London: HMSO 1988.

Paul, M., 'Can aircraft noise nuisance be measured in money?' *Oxford Economic Papers,* vol. 23 (1971), no. 3.

Pearce, D., *Cost-Benefit Analysis* (2nd ed.), London: Macmillan 1992.

Pearce, D. and Nash, C., *The Social Appraisal of Projects: a Text in Cost Benefit Analysis,* London: Macmillan 1981.

Pinches, G., 'Myopia, capital budgeting and decision making', *Financial Management,* autumn 1982, 6–19.

Pohl, G. and Mihaljek, D., 'Project evaluation and uncertainty in practice: a statistical analysis of rate-of-return divergences of 1,015 World Bank projects', *World Bank Economic Review,* vol. 6 (1992), 255–77.

Porter, M., *Competitive Strategy,* New York: Free Press 1980.

Prest, A. and Turvey, R., 'Cost-benefit analysis: a survey', *Economic Journal,* Dec. 1965.

Price Waterhouse, *Improving the Performance of Irish Tourism,* Dublin: Stationery Office 1987.

Rappaport, A. and Taggart, R., 'Evaluation of capital expenditure proposals under inflation', *Financial Management,* spring 1982, 5–13.

Ray, A., *Cost-Benefit Analysis: Issues and Methodologies,* Baltimore (Maryland): Johns Hopkins University Press 1984.

Ruane, F., 'Project analysis and industrial employment in Ireland', *ESRI Quarterly Economic Commentary,* Jun. 1979, 17–34.

Schwab, B. and Luxztig, P., 'A comparative analysis of the net present value and benefit-cost ratios as measures of the economic desirability of investments', *Journal of Finance,* Jun. 1969, 507–16.

Sharpe, W. and Cooper, G., 'Risk-return classes of New York Stock Exchange common stocks, 1931–1967', *Financial Analysts' Journal,* Mar.–Apr. 1972.

Sjaastad, L. and Weiscarver D., 'The social cost of public finance', *Journal of Political Economy,* vol. 85 (1977), no. 3.

Snower, D., 'Converting unemployment benefits into employment subsidies', *American Economic Review, Papers and Proceedings,* vol. 84 (1994), 65–71.

Spackman, M., *Discount Rates and Required Rates of Return in the Public Sector: Economic Aspects* (Working Paper no. 113), London: Government Economic Service 1991.

Squire, L., 'Project evaluation in theory and practice', in H. Chenery and T. Srinivasan (eds.), *Handbook of Development Economics,* vol. 2, Amsterdam: North Holland 1989.

Stanley, M. and Block, S., 'A survey of multinational capital budgeting', *Financial Review,* Mar. 1984, 36–51.

Stiglitz, J., *Economics of the Public Sector* (2nd ed.), Norton 1988.

Sugden, R. and Williams, A., *The Principles of Practical Cost-Benefit Analysis,* Oxford: Oxford University Press 1978.

Tansey, P., 'Whitegate oil: civil servants want closure', *Sunday Tribune,* 11 Jul. 1983.

Thaler, R. and Rosen, S., *The Value of Saving a Life: Evidence from the Labor Market* (Paper 74-2), New York: University of Rochester 1974.

Thompson, M., *Benefit Cost Analysis for Program Evaluation,* Beverley Hills (California): Sage 1980.

Turvey, R., *Optimal Pricing and Investment in Electricity Supply,* London: Allen and Unwin 1968.

Università Commerciale Luigi Bocconi, *MEANS: Methods for Evaluating Structural Policies: the Pescara Marina (Abrizzo): a Cost-Benefit Analysis,* Brussels: CEOPS and Commission of the European Communities 1994.

US Congress, Joint Economic Committee, *The Analysis and Evaluation of Public Expenditures: the PPB System,* vol. 1, Washington: Government Printing Office 1969.

Weinstein, M., Shepard, D. and Pilskin, J., 'The economic value of changing mortality probabilities: a decision theoretic approach', *Quarterly Journal of Economics,* vol. 94 (1980), 373–96.

Woodbury, S. and Spiegelman, R., 'Bonuses to workers and employers to reduce unemployment: randomized trials in Illinois', *American Economic Review,* vol. 77 (1987), 513–30.

Yellen, J., 'Efficiency wage models of unemployment', *American Economic Review,* vol. 74 (1984), 200–205.

INDEX